GOVERNMENT IN CRISIS

GOVERNMENT IN CRISIS

WHAT EVERY AMERICAN SHOULD KNOW ABOUT THE FEDERAL BUDGET DEFICIT

David Brashear

Chesapeake River Press
Alexandria, Virginia

339.5230973
B82g

Copyright © 1991 by David Brashear
All rights reserved. No part of the contents of this book may be reproduced or
transmitted in any form or by any means without the written permission of the
publisher.

Library of Congress Catalog Card Number: 91-072564

ISBN 0-9629694-9-4

Printed and bound in the United States of America.

Published by:
    Chesapeake River Press
    P.O. Box 19141
    Alexandria, Virginia 22320

For Judy, Jan, and Laurie

University Libraries
Carnegie Mellon University
Pittsburgh, PA 15213-3890

CONTENTS

PREFACE

The Federal budget deficit in 1990 was almost $277 billion. On December 31, 1990, the accumulated debt incurred by the Federal Government, but not yet repaid, stood at $3.37 trillion. Each day, the Government pays hundreds of millions of dollars in interest on its debt balance. How have we managed to get ourselves into this situation?

What is most notable about today's Federal deficits is the context in which they arose. The 1980s were a period of economic prosperity and success in the United States - the country was able to put the oil shocks of the 1970s into its past. Once the recession of the early 1980s was reversed, a long economic expansion began. Per capita disposable personal income rose from $8,421 in 1980 to $15,191 in 1989, an increase of 80%. Purchasing power expanded as Federal income tax rates on individuals fell and the efforts to control inflation paid off.

Unfortunately, the prosperity and fiscal stability that prevailed in many American households in the 1980s was not shared by the Federal Government. New economic growth theories were tested by bureaucrats in Washington, and Federal spending began to increase at a dramatic rate.

The result has been a severe, and continuing, revenue shortfall. The deficit in the budget of the Federal Government ballooned after the recession of the early 1980s and the tax cut and military buildup of the

Reagan Administration. Since that time, the Federal Government has been unable to bring the annual budget back to a near-balance position.

The recurring budget deficit is large, and growing, and the accumulated Federal deficit is enormous, but it does not seem to worry many people. Few politicians have demonstrated much interest in solving the problem. And the voting public, taking its cue from elected officials, has not been outspoken on deficit matters.

But the budget situation is a problem that should be of great concern to all of us. The dollars being spent are real dollars, and must eventually be paid by real taxes - *our* taxes. Furthermore, the quantities of money being dismissed as mere deficits are so sizable that they are almost inconceivable.

Much of the Government's inaction on the budget deficit stems from the politicians' belief that electorate apathy will always prevail when the budget is mentioned. This attitude is apparent within some wings of the White House and the U.S. Capitol. The electorate apathy is purported to spring from the inability of most citizens to comprehend the multi-faceted Federal budget - "what they can't understand can't upset them."

I believe that an understanding of the mammoth Federal operation is within the grasp of all interested citizens. Additionally, it should be important to all citizens, because the budget decisions of the 1990s will affect America for decades to come.

In this book, I attempt to draw parallels between various aspects of the Federal Government and its finances and other more widely known information. I make many comparisons, some almost outlandishly conceived, to try to illustrate my arguments. As often as it is possible, I convey critical pieces of information in graphical form. At the end of each chapter, I present a series of questions called Opinion Builders. The book concludes with an exercise entitled "Balance the Budget Yourself." My motivation is to inform the public and draw out opinion. My hope is that, armed with a new base of knowledge and understanding, the American electorate can ask its representatives the tough questions when confronted with their bids for reelection.

I don't subscribe to the notion that there can be a Republican or Democratic solution to the budget imbalance. I am convinced that the only intelligent resolution lies in a fresh approach, combining elements of both conservative and liberal policy.

Consequently, I have intended to construct a non-partisan picture of the current budgetary problem. I have not attempted to educate the reader with my theories for how the situation could be changed, and I hope that I have been successful.

The electorate must take leadership on the budget issue, for we have been failed by our elected representatives. It's up to all of us - it is our civic responsibility.

CHAPTER ONE

OVERVIEW OF THE FEDERAL GOVERNMENT

Past, Present, and Future

The mismatch of Federal revenues and expenses took on a new dimension in the 1980s. Government spending grew to new and unprecedented levels. Today, the total annual spending of our Federal Government is so great that it exceeds the entire economic output of France. In other words, if all of the production and output of the French economy were used to pay for the operation of the Federal Government of the United States, there would not be enough funds to meet all of the Federal expenses mandated by current law. France is a convenient example, but why single out just one country? The Federal Government's expenditures exceed the Gross National Product (GNP) of Great Britain, Italy, Brazil, Canada, Spain, and most other nations. Only three countries - the Soviet Union, Japan, and Germany - have economies that are larger than the U.S. Federal Government. However, this has not always been true.

The Federal Government in the United States has evolved considerably since its founding. The framers of the Constitution envisioned a relatively weak central government, much different from that which existed in most of Europe at the time. The emphasis in political debate and adopted law was on the rights of the individual states, combined almost secondarily with the need for some central governing mechanism to tie the various states together. To further protect against

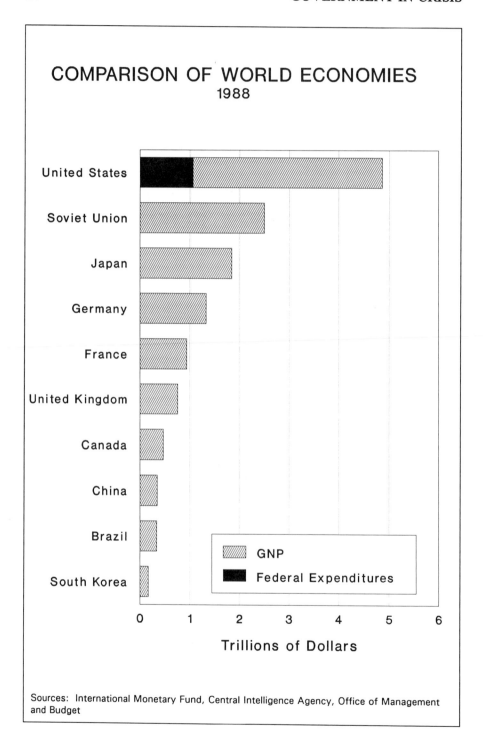

COMPARISON OF WORLD ECONOMIES
1988

Trillions of Dollars

GNP
Federal Expenditures

Sources: International Monetary Fund, Central Intelligence Agency, Office of Management and Budget

centralized power, the Constitution provided for the establishment of three separate branches in the Federal Government. The checks and balances created between the Executive, Legislative, and Judicial branches are known to all who have studied the American political process.

As the complexity of society advanced in the nineteenth and twentieth centuries, the power and scope of the Federal Government grew to be substantially larger than that which was envisioned by our forefathers. To better represent and service a growing constituency, the Legislative and Judicial Branches have grown considerably. However, the range of responsibilities for these two branches has not significantly changed. The missions of both the Legislature and the Judiciary remain more purely linked to creating and interpreting the law, while the role of the Executive Branch has stretched beyond that which had been planned by the authors of the Constitution.

The expansion of the responsibility of the Executive Branch has been much more extensive than that of its sister branches, and with that expansion the power of the Presidency has increased. In addition to the growth of Cabinet-level departments which oversee the commerce, finances, social welfare, natural resources, and national defense of the country, the Executive Branch now includes many agencies with surprisingly specific agendas.

Today, the Federal Government is an enormous operation. In 1990, it employed over three million people in civilian positions. In addition, just over two million individuals were active-duty, full time members of one of the national branches of the military. In all, 1 of every 30 working-age Americans was employed by the Federal Government in 1990.

The Federal Government regularly touches the lives of every American citizen. It is nearly impossible for an individual citizen not to explicitly benefit from some part of the Federal operation on a daily basis. Much of the transportation infrastructure that exists in the U.S., including highways, airports, and mass transit systems, has been constructed with the help of Federal monies. Federal programs provide medical insurance, income assistance, and social security. A number of

THE U.S. GOVERNMENT

(as of June 1989)

```
                    THE
                CONSTITUTION
```

LEGISLATIVE BRANCH	EXECUTIVE BRANCH	JUDICIAL BRANCH
THE CONGRESS	**THE PRESIDENT**	**THE SUPREME COURT**
Senate House	**Executive Office of the President**	
Architect of the Capitol U.S. Botanic Garden General Accounting Office Government Printing Office Library of Congress Office of Technology Assessment Congressional Budget Office Copyright Royalty Tribunal U.S. Tax Court	White House Office Office of Management & Budget Council of Economic Advisors National Security Council Office of Policy Development Office of the United States Trade Representative National Critical Materials Council Council on Environmental Quality Office of Science & Technology Policy Office of Administration Office of National Drug Control Policy National Space Council THE VICE PRESIDENT Cabinet Level Departments Quasi-independent Government Agencies and Corporations	U.S. Courts of Appeals U.S. District Courts U.S. Claims Court U.S. Court of Appeals for the Federal Circuit U.S. Court of International Trade Territorial Courts U.S. Court of Military Appeals Administrative Court of the United States Courts Federal Judicial Center

Source: Bureau of
         the Census

cultural programs are run by the Federal Government, such as the National Endowment for the Arts and the Smithsonian Institution. The extensive system of National Parks is owned, managed, and maintained by the Federal Government through the Department of the Interior. And space exploration and defense-related research have spawned many of the technological breakthroughs of the twentieth century.

THE ACRONYM GAME

How many agencies and offices of the Federal Government can you identify by commonly used acronyms?

1. AID	11. FEC	21. NASA
2. CBO	12. FEMA	22. NHTSA
3. CIA	13. FTC	23. NIH
4. DOD	14. GAO	24. NLRB
5. DOE	15. GNMA	25. NRC
6. EPA	16. GPO	26. OSHA
7. FAA	17. GSA	27. SBA
8. FBI	18. HUD	28. SEC
9. FCC	19. ICC	29. TVA
10. FDIC	20. ITC	30. USIA

Answers: 1. Agency for International Development; 2. Congressional Budget Office; 3. Central Intelligence Agency; 4. Department of Defense; 5. Department of Energy; 6. Environmental Protection Agency; 7. Federal Aviation Administration; 8. Federal Bureau of Investigation; 9. Federal Communications Commission; 10. Federal Deposit Insurance Corporation; 11. Federal Election Commission; 12. Federal Emergency Management Agency; 13. Federal Trade Commission; 14. General Accounting Office; 15. Government National Mortgage Association; 16. Government Printing Office; 17. General Services Administration; 18. Department of Housing and Urban Development; 19. Interstate Commerce Commission; 20. International Trade Commission; 21. National Aeronautics and Space Administration; 22. National Highway Traffic Safety Administration; 23. National Institutes of Health; 24. National Labor Relations Board; 25. Nuclear Regulatory Commission; 26. Occupational Safety and Health Administration; 27. Small Business Administration; 28. Securities and Exchange Commission; 29. Tennessee Valley Authority; 30. United States Information Agency.

THE OPERATIONS OF THE CABINET-LEVEL DEPARTMENTS OF

AGRICULTURE:
  Agricultural Research Service
  Cooperative State Research Service
  Extension Service
  National Agricultural Library
  National Agricultural Statistical Service
  Foreign Assistance Programs
  Agricultural Stabilization & Conservation Service
  Federal Crop Insurance Corporation
  Commodity Credit Corporation
  Rural Electrification Administration
  Farmers Home Administration
  Soil Conservation Service
  Animal & Plant Health Inspection Service
  Food Safety & Inspection Service
  Food & Nutrition Service

COMMERCE:
  Economic Development Administration
  National Institute of Standards & Technology
  Bureau of the Census
  International Trade Administration
  Minority Business Development Agency
  United States Travel & Tourism Administration
  National Oceanic & Atmospheric Administration
  Patent and Trademark Office

DEFENSE:
  Army
  Navy
  Air Force
  Marine Corps

EDUCATION:
  Office of Special Education & Rehabilitative Services
  Office of Elementary & Secondary Education
  Office of Bilingual Education & Minority Language Affairs
  Office of Vocational & Adult Education
  Office of Postsecondary Education
  Office of Educational Research & Improvement

ENERGY:
  Atomic Energy Defense Activities
  Power Marketing Administration
  Strategic Petroleum Reserve
  Federal Energy Regulatory Commission
  Nuclear Waste Disposal Fund

HEALTH AND HUMAN SERVICES:
  Food and Drug Administration
  Health Resources & Services Administration
  Indian Health Service
  Centers for Disease Control
  National Institutes of Health
  Family Support Administration
  Health Care Financing Administration
  Social Security Administration
  Alcohol, Drug Abuse & Mental Health Administration

THE EXECUTIVE BRANCH OF THE FEDERAL GOVERNMENT

HOUSING AND URBAN DEVELOPMENT:
  Public & Indian Housing Programs
  Government National Mortgage Association
  Community Planning & Development

INTERIOR:
  Bureau of Land Management
  Minerals Management Service
  Office of Surface Mining Reclamation & Enforcement
  Bureau of Reclamation
  Geological Survey
  Bureau of Mines
  U.S. Fish & Wildlife Service
  National Park Service
  Bureau of Indian Affairs
  Territorial & International Affairs

JUSTICE:
  U.S. Parole Commission
  Federal Bureau of Investigation
  Drug Enforcement Administration
  Immigration & Naturalization Service
  Federal Prison System

LABOR:
  Employment & Training Administration
  Pension Benefit Guaranty Corporation
  Employment Standards Administration
  Occupational Safety & Health Administration
  Mine Safety & Health Administration
  Bureau of Labor Statistics

STATE:
  Administration of Foreign Affairs

TRANSPORTATION:
  Federal Highway Administration
  Federal Railroad Administration
  Urban Mass Transit Administration
  National Highway Traffic Safety Administration
  Federal Aviation Administration
  Coast Guard
  Maritime Administration

TREASURY:
  Financial Management Service
  Federal Law Enforcement Training Center
  Bureau of Alcohol, Tobacco & Firearms
  U.S. Customs Service
  U.S. Mint
  Internal Revenue Service
  U.S. Secret Service
  Office of Thrift Supervision

VETERANS AFFAIRS:
  Veterans Benefits Administration
  Veterans Health Services & Research Administration

Source: Office of Management and Budget

The Federal Government is pervasive and its activities costly, but its goal is to positively stimulate the economy. The financial basics of the Government's operations follow a business paradigm: revenues are offset by expenses, resulting in either a surplus or a deficit. When a deficit is recorded, the Government does not pay for it by simply printing more money - that would fuel inflation. Rather, it uses another method to bridge the deficit gap. In effect, the Federal Government has its own "credit card", and can "charge" deficits, which accumulate and can be carried for years. An annual revenue shortfall is only a problem until the Treasury has had enough time to sell Treasury bonds. By printing and selling these bonds, the Government collects money from individuals and financial institutions in the amount of the face value of the bonds. This money is in turn used to make up for the shortfall in tax revenues. The bonds represent an ongoing obligation, for which the Government must pay its "lenders" a periodic interest payment.

Whether or not the Federal budget should be in balance on an annual basis is widely debated. Some economists say that the name of the game is to balance the budget (i.e. make revenues = expenses), now and for eternity. Other economists willingly accept a recurring annual deficit because it represents the efforts of the Government to stimulate the economy. There are virtually no known supporters for a continuing surplus - that would mean taxing people above the necessary rate. Interestingly, the only time in the last 30 years that the Federal budget balanced was in 1969. In that year, the Government recorded a small surplus, due in part to a non-recurring individual income tax surcharge, a permanent increase in the rate of the Social Security tax, and a temporary slowdown in overall spending growth.

After 1969, the annual "bottom-line" of the Federal Government began a long and steady deterioration. Actual deficits became more significant, both relatively and absolutely. Tax reform in the 1980s constrained the ability of the Federal Government to raise revenues, and required the Treasury Department to sell a large amount of bonds to finance the revenue shortfall. The annual interest obligations on these outstanding bonds has become a heavy burden, representing over 15% of total Federal expenditures in 1990. A continuing increase of debt and debt service such as this is unsustainable.

The direction the Government will take in the future is not yet clear. The general public demands the services provided by the Federal Government, which are considerable in cost. Regulatory functions performed by the Government sustain progress and maintain order in our society. Where is the line drawn between necessary services and those which the country could function without, but at a lesser degree of comfort, contentment or quality of life for its citizens? Trimming department budgets and eliminating programs are difficult tasks to accomplish, and legislation enacting new taxes can have painful side effects for officials who advocate such changes.

OPINION BUILDERS

1. *Our founding fathers sought a weak central government. Has such a concept become unworkable, given the complexity of modern society, or is a weak central government a desirable and appropriate governing philosophy?*

2. *Has the Federal Government assumed too broad a role in the day-to-day life of twentieth century America, or is it providing needed regulation and services?*

3. *Are you able to identify the benefits provided by the Federal Government that you rely upon on a daily basis? Are these services necessary to your daily existence, and worthy of the tax burden that they represent?*

4. *Would you support the elimination of a Federal subsidy, such as for public transportation, that directly affected your community?*

5. *Do you believe that the continuing Federal budget deficit is a cause worthy of concern?*

CHAPTER TWO

LARGE NUMBERS IN PERSPECTIVE

How to Take a Billion Dollars Seriously

The Federal Government now receives and disburses well over one trillion dollars annually. Billions of dollars are spent on hundreds of different programs. So before we immerse ourselves in the Federal budget cauldron, it is important to spend time grasping the magnitude of these numbers.

Let's first get a grounding in the understanding of large numbers by exploring the concept of one million. In the world today, many statistics are expressed in quantities described as millions. There are wealthy millionaires, "Million Dollar Sales Honors", and lottery jackpots promising countless millions. We hear about "millions" so often, in fact, that many of us develop an insensitivity to what the amount really represents. We become users of the "million" term without really contemplating its grand scale.

Exploring human populations is a good place to start the quest of conceptualizing "millions." Some states in the U.S. do not even have populations numbering in the millions, including some of the largest states in terms of land area, such as Alaska, Montana, and Wyoming. A hypothetical census will enable us to use population statistics further. If a one-year national census of the population were being conducted, and each employee were responsible for questioning and tabulating short responses from 10,000 people in that time (or approximately 40 per working day), then 25,000 employees would be necessary to accomplish the census project for the entire United States. The same exercise in China would require over 110,000 employees, and over 85,000 in India.

Distance examples are another way of comprehending larger numbers. Imagine that a highway has been built around the Earth at the equator, spanning oceans and crossing land. Its length would be approximately 25,000 miles. If a person set out to drive one million miles on that highway, it would require circling the globe approximately 40 times. If the driver sustained an average speed of 55 miles per hour, travelling 16 hours per day, it would take almost 38 months to complete the journey (i.e. over 3 years). If one flew a large aircraft, rather than drove, but still logged one million miles, it would take 83 solid days of flying at a speed of 500 miles per hour to reach the goal.

Billions are even more intimidating than millions. Once again, statistics can better illustrate the actual quantity. A production example is a good place to start. In the history of U.S. automobile manufacturing, spanning over 80 years, the total production of passenger cars has not exceeded one billion. That includes the Chevrolets that your great grandfather owned, the Plymouths purchased by your grandmother, and the Fords that were driven by your parents.

Another population example demonstrates the power of billions. Imagine that all of the countries in the European Economic Community (currently numbering 12) decided to turn their land into one large wild animal reserve. Through a negotiated agreement, all of the citizens were to emigrate to the United States. Despite the huge immigration into America that would result, the population of the U.S. would still be substantially less than one billion - or approximately 600 million. Our newly populated country would still only have 52% of the population of China. In fact, the number of human beings living on this planet is estimated at only 5.3 billion in 1990.

Clearly, one billion is a tremendous quantity. A discussion of one billion in money terms should further highlight the dramatic number about which we are talking.

For our first example, we will work with automobiles. Assume that an average automobile sells for $12,000. In such a scenario, $1 billion would be enough money to purchase 83,000 cars. This would provide a new car to every family in Rochester, New York.

Alternatively, if a two-week dream vacation to Europe costs $2,000, an account having a balance of $1 billion would be enough to send 500,000 people on that vacation. Such a trip could include the entire population of Denver, Colorado, and would result in the need for more than 1,300 747 flights to transport the travelers. If the travelers were all landing at Charles de Gaulle airport in Paris, with a plane landing every five minutes, it would take more than 4 days to place all of the travelers on French soil.

HOW LARGE CAN A NUMBER BE?	
Ten Thousand	10,000
One Hundred Thousand	100,000
One Million	1,000,000
One Hundred Million	100,000,000
One Billion	1,000,000,000
One Hundred Billion	100,000,000,000
One Trillion	1,000,000,000,000

Imagine that the Federal Government decided that the surveillance of all Americans was important, and so it would provide $125 cameras to as many citizens as possible to photograph their compatriots. If the budget for the purchase of these cameras was $1 billion, then 8 million Americans could be armed with such a photographic capability.

A substantial quantity of food can be purchased for $1 billion. Consider the following question. How much would it cost to provide a $1.50 snack, consisting of an apple, a bag of chips, a candy bar and a can of juice to every human being on earth? The entire population of the world, from India to Indiana, could enjoy that one day snack for $8 billion.

Now we are ready for numbers of the size that are found in something like the Federal budget. Take the earlier automobile example, but adjust it for more substantial quantities. We find that a $100 billion account would be enough to buy one of our new cars for more than 8.3 million families, or almost 10% of all families living in the U.S. In fact, $100 billion would buy 10 gallons of gasoline every week of the year for 153 million cars.

Today's Federal budget has gone even beyond billions. Federal analysts talk not of billions, but trillions. Few statistics quoted in modern society need to invoke a number as substantial, particularly when dealing with items of man's creation. One trillion dollars is a quantity so large that relevant examples are difficult to find.

It takes a monumental effort to produce $1 trillion worth of economic value. The total sales of the top 32 industrial companies listed in the *Fortune 500* in 1989 was approximately $1 trillion, which includes the likes of General Motors, Exxon, IBM, Boeing, Procter and Gamble, and Westinghouse. To accumulate the next $1 trillion of industrial sales from that list, however, it would be necessary to count the sales of the next 285 largest corporations.

The power of $1 trillion can be demonstrated through the distribution of capital and the resulting widespread wealth. If the Federal Government were to decide to create millionaires by handing out envelopes containing $1 million, a trillion dollars would permit officials to hand out one million of these envelopes, thereby creating one million new millionaires. If they were spread evenly throughout the fifty states, each state could expect to record 20,000 new families as millionaire families.

INDUSTRIAL POWER
The Largest American Corporations - 1989

1.	General Motors	$127.0 B	17.	United Technologies	$19.8 B
2.	Ford Motor	96.9	18.	Eastman Kodak	18.4
3.	Exxon	86.7	19.	USX	17.8
4.	IBM	63.4	20.	Dow Chemical	17.7
5.	General Electric	55.3	21.	Xerox	17.6
6.	Mobil	51.0	22.	Atlantic Richfield	15.9
7.	Philip Morris	39.1	23.	Pepsico	15.4
8.	Chrysler	36.2	24.	RJR Nabisco	15.2
9.	Du Pont	35.2	25.	McDonnell Douglas	15.0
10.	Texaco	32.4	26.	Tenneco	14.4
11.	Chevron	29.4	27.	Digital Equipment	12.9
12.	Amoco	24.2	28.	Westinghouse	12.8
13.	Shell Oil	21.7	29.	Rockwell	12.6
14.	Procter & Gamble	21.7	30.	Phillips Petroleum	12.5
15.	Boeing	20.3	31.	Allied Signal	12.0
16.	Occidental Petroleum	20.1	32.	3M	12.0

Total Revenues of the 32 Largest Industrials: $1,002.6 Billion

Note: Fiscal years vary among companies.
Source: <u>Fortune</u>

One trillion dollars is enough to buy a new $12,000 automobile for almost every American family in 1990.

Finally, instead of encouraging oil consumption, one trillion dollars could be used for school tuition. If every American citizen between the ages of 5 and 24 were to be granted tuition money out of an evenly divided $1 trillion scholarship fund, each would get approximately $14,000 to pay for educational costs. The possibilities of what might come from such an expenditure are staggering.

Now that we have refreshed our appreciation for millions, billions, and trillions, we can move away from hypothetical examples and take a closer look at the real thing: the operations of our national government. Forget about hundreds and thousands - in Federal parlance those figures are rounding errors. Concentrate on billions and trillions. The current budget projections for 1992 show the U.S. spending almost $1.5 trillion in that fiscal year alone, while also collecting over $1 trillion from taxpayers. It is hard to believe that the Federal Government could collect and spend so much money in just one year, but its true.

CHAPTER THREE

THE REVENUES OF THE FEDERAL GOVERNMENT

Feeding the Big Machine

Just as it is difficult to exist in the U.S. on a day-to-day basis without benefitting from some Federal resource, it is also nearly impossible to carry on a normal day without paying something to the Federal Government by way of taxes. The Federal Government's tax hand reaches far: we pay income taxes, social insurance taxes, and consumption taxes.

One of the major issues that prompted the start of the Revolutionary War was the imposition of taxes by officials who had not been elected to represent the people. When the Constitution of the United States was finally drafted and approved, it was the elected and representative Congress that was given the power of taxation, ending an era of taxation without representation. The first two powers granted to Congress in Article I, Section VIII of the Constitution are particularly important:

The Congress shall have Power:

> *To lay and collect Taxes, Duties, Imposts and Excises, to pay the Debts and provide for the common Defense and general Welfare of the United States; but all*

*Duties, Imposts and excises shall be uniform throughout
the United States;*

To borrow Money on the Credit of the United States....

For most of our nation's first 135 years, revenues came from two
sources which would surprise modern Americans.   The colonists
inherited a country with little industrial infrastructure. As new industries
developed, they were typically weak and vulnerable, and required
protection from foreign competition. The first major tax was a tariff on
imports, which was varied from time to time to meet the needs of
developing American industries and the U.S. Government. The second
major revenue source stemmed from the geographic expansion of the
U.S. Large amounts of land became Federal property through various
purchases and wars, and by confiscating it from Indian tribes. The sale
of this land, primarily in the mid-to-late 1800s, was a steady source of
Federal revenue.

The Current System of Taxation

In modern times, it is easy to see that Congress has mightily
embraced the powers of taxation granted by the founding fathers. In
1990, Congress levied and collected taxes totalling $1,031 billion, or
approximately $4,125 for each and every citizen of the United States.
And Congress has also become very adept at borrowing money on the
credit of the United States - over $3.3 trillion of debt was outstanding on
January 1, 1991. Each year a budget deficit is recorded, the Government
must borrow more and add to the level of outstanding debt.

The Federal Government employs two different types of taxes -
progressive and flat. In a progressive tax structure, a given tax is higher
for those individuals or entities which earn more. In a flat tax structure,
the rate of taxation is uniform for all. Congress chooses between these
types each time it restructures the tax system. There are inherent social
policy considerations and implications involved.   For example,
progressive taxes such as the income tax result in some income
redistribution. Flat taxes, like those on alcohol or cigarettes, may have
the onus of a penalty for consumption of these items and indicate a

certain element of behavior control. Flat taxes can often be considered regressive, as is the case with the tax on the consumption of gasoline. Take, for example, two individuals who both use 500 gallons of gasoline per year to drive to work. However, one earns $15,000 a year while the other earns $100,000. Though the actual dollars spent on gas taxes are identical, the higher earning individual pays a lower percentage of his income for the gasoline tax than does the person earning less money.

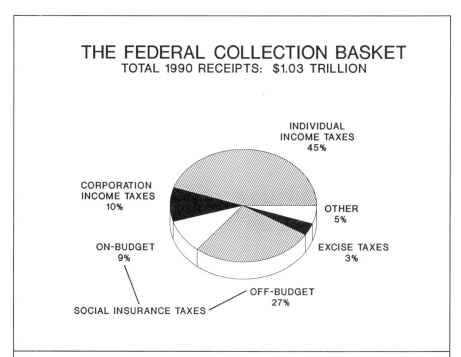

THE FEDERAL COLLECTION BASKET
TOTAL 1990 RECEIPTS: $1.03 TRILLION

INDIVIDUAL INCOME TAXES 45%

CORPORATION INCOME TAXES 10%

OTHER 5%

ON-BUDGET 9%

EXCISE TAXES 3%

OFF-BUDGET 27%

SOCIAL INSURANCE TAXES

Note: Social Insurance Taxes are categorized as being either off-budget or on-budget. Off-budget receipts include taxes and contributions for Old Age and Survivors Insurance and Disability Insurance (collectively referred to as Social Security). On-budget receipts include taxes and contributions for railroad retirement programs, Federal employees' retirement programs, and unemployment insurance programs.

Source: Office of Management and Budget

While income taxes in the U.S. have tended to be progressive, the remaining portion of Federal revenues are generally flat taxes. The FICA tax (Social Security) is a flat tax imposed upon earnings below an annually adjusted threshold. Excise taxes are another group of flat taxes imposed by the Federal Government, and are typically targeted at consumption, including taxes such as the gasoline tax and the cigarette tax. These taxes are paid according to amounts purchased: per gallon in the case of the gasoline tax; per pack in the case of the cigarette tax.

Individual Income Taxes

A large portion of the revenues raised by the Federal Government comes from income taxes. Personal income taxes accounted for 45% of revenues raised in fiscal 1990. However, they have not always existed in this country. The first income tax was enacted in 1862 to assist in the financing of the Civil War, but was repealed in 1872. Twenty-two years later, the Congress passed a revenue act which once again established an individual income tax, but it was very unpopular among the eastern financial community. This tax was challenged and quickly abolished by the Supreme Court in 1895, when it was found to be in conflict with the Constitution.

Clearly, a change in the Constitution was necessary to allow for the existence of a national income tax. The 16th Amendment to the Constitution was proposed by Congress on July 12, 1909, and ratified on February 25, 1913. The 16th Amendment states:

The Congress shall have power to lay and collect taxes on incomes, from whatever source derived, without apportion- ment among the several States, and without regard to any census or enumeration.

Once the 16th Amendment was ratified, the Congress reestablished the individual income tax as part of the Revenue Act of 1913, and the Federal income tax has been in place ever since.

Today's income tax is substantially different from that which existed prior to the legislation of the 1980s. In 1981, early in the first Reagan administration, a sweeping reform was made to the individual income tax. It was an effort to ease the burden of personal taxes, rectify the bracket creep that had been caused by inflation in the late 1970s and early 1980s, and reestablish the incentive for Americans to earn as much as they could. General tax rates were dropped 25%, with the reduction phased in over three years. In addition, the top tax bracket was reduced from 70 percent to 50 percent. More recently, the highest marginal tax rate on individuals' incomes has been reduced even further, and in 1991 stands at 31%.

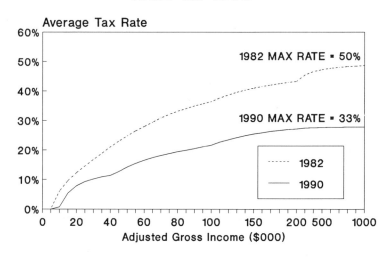

THE REFORM OF THE PERSONAL INCOME TAX IN THE 1980s MADE IT MUCH LESS PROGRESSIVE THAN IT HAD BEEN IN THE PAST

1982 vs. 1990

Assumptions: Rates are based on tax paid for a given level of income, as measured by the IRS definition of Adjusted Gross Income. Calculations assume married couple filing jointly, with no dependent children. Two exemptions are included. Calculation does not incorporate any itemized deductions, but includes the standard deduction for 1990.

Note: Max rate listed for each year is maximum marginal tax rate on tax rate schedule.

Source: Internal Revenue Service

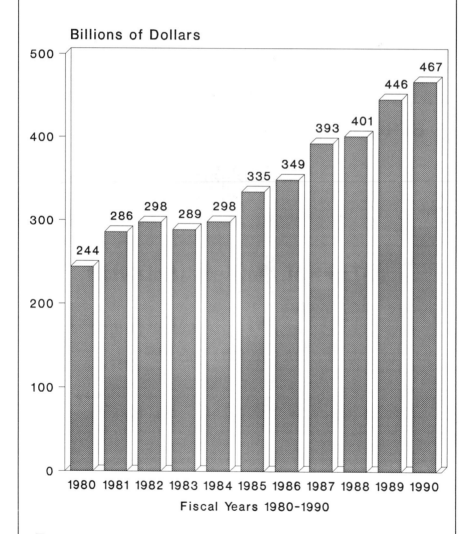

DESPITE THE REDUCTION IN TAX RATES,
TOTAL PERSONAL INCOME TAX RECEIPTS ROSE
IN THE 1980s AS THE ECONOMY EXPANDED

PERSONAL INCOME TAX RECEIPTS

Billions of Dollars

Fiscal Years 1980-1990

Source: Office of Management and Budget

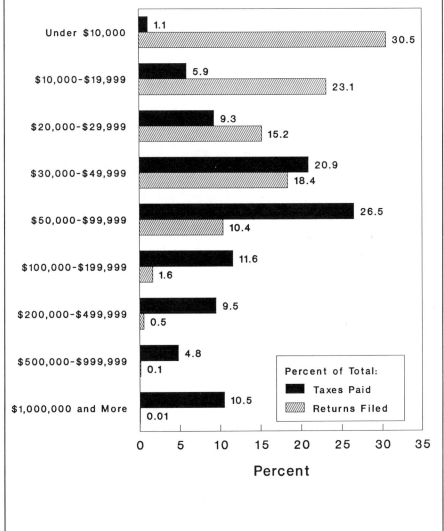

WHO PAYS THE FEDERAL INCOME TAX?
% OF TOTAL INDIVIDUAL INCOME TAXES PAID
BY EACH INCOME GROUP
1988 Estimates

Income:

Income	Taxes Paid	Returns Filed
Under $10,000	1.1	30.5
$10,000-$19,999	5.9	23.1
$20,000-$29,999	9.3	15.2
$30,000-$49,999	20.9	18.4
$50,000-$99,999	26.5	10.4
$100,000-$199,999	11.6	1.6
$200,000-$499,999	9.5	0.5
$500,000-$999,999	4.8	0.1
$1,000,000 and More	10.5	0.01

Percent of Total:
■ Taxes Paid
▨ Returns Filed

Percent
0 5 10 15 20 25 30 35

Source: Internal Revenue Service

Corporate Income Taxes

An income tax on corporate profits has been levied since 1909. The initial tax rates imposed on corporate earnings were very small, but over the years the rates have been raised to over 50% from time to time.

Corporate profits are unique because they are subject to Federal taxes twice, a double jeopardy of sorts for successful operations. At the corporate level, all profits are subject to Federal taxation, at the rate of approximately 34% for most large companies at the current time. If those profits are then distributed to shareholders in the form of a dividend, such dividends are again taxable on personal income tax returns as additional ordinary income.

THE CORPORATE INCOME TAX IS A MAJOR
REVENUE SOURCE, BUT IT IS SOMETIMES
SUBJECT TO ECONOMIC CONDITIONS

CORPORATE INCOME TAX RECEIPTS

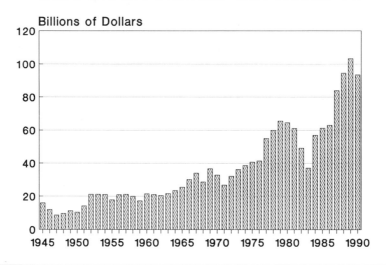

Notes: Excludes Transition Quarter (TQ), July - September, 1976, left out when fiscal year was shifted. Beginning in 1987, includes minor trust fund receipts for the hazardous substance superfund.

Source: Office of Management and Budget

Company profits vary depending on the economic climate. A long or severe recession can substantially reduce the total level of corporate profits in the economy, and consequently have an impact on the revenue side of the Federal budget. The total of corporate income taxes received in fiscal year 1983, a relatively poor time for the economy, was $37 billion. That amount was only slightly larger than the amount collected in fiscal year 1969, and less than the total corporate income taxes paid in 1974.

FICA Tax

A series of trust funds administered by the Federal Government provide the social welfare safety net, including Old Age and Survivors Income (Social Security), Medicare, and Disability Income. Social Security and Medicare beneficiaries are primarily of retirement age, although other individuals with certain disabilities and family situations can qualify for benefits.

The FICA tax on wages is the sole source of income from which benefits are paid for Social Security, Medicare, or Disability Insurance. This tax is withheld from every taxpayer's paycheck, and the sums can be significant. The tax is flat, and has grown substantially in size since its inception during the Roosevelt Administration. The trust funds maintain positive balances from year to year, so that any fluctuations in receipts can be easily absorbed, without interruption of the payment of benefits.

The combined FICA tax paid into the funds is 15.3% of each employee's earnings. Fifty percent comes out of the employee's paycheck, and the remainder is matched by the employer. Self-employed individuals must pay the full 15.3% themselves, compensating for the lack of the employer portion. In 1991, the FICA tax is paid on a maximum wage base of $53,400 for Social Security and Disability Insurance. The portion of the tax for Medicare is paid on a total wage base of $125,000 in 1991. All maximum wage bases on which these taxes are levied are indexed for inflation, which means they increase each year by the reported rate of inflation (similar to a cost-of-living adjustment, or COLA).

Federal Excise Taxes

The Federal Government has enacted a wide range of excise taxes. These taxes are sometimes called consumption taxes or user taxes, and are imposed on the production, sale or consumption of certain goods, foodstuffs, and services. Some excise taxes are imposed at specific

---

FEDERAL EXCISE TAX RECEIPTS - 1990
($ million)

Federal Funds:	
Alcohol taxes	5,695
Tobacco taxes	4,081
Telephone use taxes	2,995
Other	2,820
Total	15,591
Trust Funds:	
Highways	13,867
Airports/Airways	3,700
Black Lung	665
Inland Waterway	63
Hazardous Substances	
Response	818
Post Closure Liability	-1
Aquatic Resources	218
Leaking Underground	
Storage Tank	122
Oil Spill Liability	143
Vaccine Injury	
Compensation	159
Total	19,754
Total Excise Taxes	35,345

Note: Excise tax receipts are deposited into either the Federal funds account or a specific trust fund account. Federal Funds are generally available for expenditure by any Government agency for any approved item. Trust fund monies are specifically set aside to fund specific projects related to the nature of the tax levied.

Source: Office of Management and Budget

rates, and some excise taxes are imposed at ad valorem rates (at a percentage of the selling price of the manufacturer). In 1989, the Federal Government raised $34.1 billion in revenues through the imposition of a myriad of excise taxes.

Excise taxes are collected for a variety of reasons. The Government claims that some are collected to compensate for the use of a Government service, benefit, or resource, such as the 10% tax on airline tickets applied in part to the upkeep of the nation's air transportation infrastructure. Others are collected to discourage certain activities, such as the vice taxes on alcohol and cigarettes. In many instances, however, excise taxes exist because of their ease of enactment.

Issues in Taxation Policy

The overall tax burden for an individual American depends upon many things, including income, wealth, and consumption. At various points in history, this overall level of taxation has been alternately described as high and low (most often high).

In today's tax environment, a stronger argument could probably be made that the tax burden an individual is asked to bear is very fair, if not even somewhat less than might reasonably be expected. This is primarily the result of the simplification and reduction of rates in the Federal individual income tax system, which constitutes the most significant part of most people's annual remittance of taxes.

The income tax reforms of the 1980s dramatically changed the way the Federal Government approached personal taxation. The new tax law marked an abrupt end to the tax system that had been evolving since the end of World War II. Rather than being composed of a plethora of tax brackets, the hallmark of a progressive tax system, the current tax code is simple and contains only a few low brackets. The top marginal income tax rate stands at its lowest level in decades.

Few topics can arouse the interest of the electorate as easily as taxes. Unfortunately, this fact lies at the center of some of the most important Federal problems we face today. While other taxes are more easily altered, proposed income tax changes are usually quickly embroiled in a political firestorm. Consequently, major changes to the personal income tax system are infrequent.

Corporate taxes are a different story. These taxes are raised and lowered periodically, with various incentive programs added and deleted along the way. Generally, business lobbies work hard to prevent the changes to the corporate tax code which result in higher levels of business taxation. But at the same time, at least one ear of any legislator is always tuned to the voice of the voting public. No legislator can ignore the fury generated when the electorate perceives that businesses are not carrying a fair share of the tax burden. And when Government revenues fall short of expenditures, a cry is heard at the grass-roots level for increases in taxes on businesses.

Despite the ease with which business taxes are levied, the impact of such taxes must always be analyzed carefully by the Government. Excessive taxation of business can undermine the strength of individual entities, and put the entire national economic system in peril. While corporations are a virtual gold mine for tax dollars, they are also a source of needed jobs, and the equation must be balanced in both directions.

Perhaps the most acceptable of all tax changes are those related to excise taxes. The political arena is often more hospitable to the establishment or increase of a small excise tax than it would be to an increase in the income tax rate. In fact, when Congress and the President finally came to agreement on a budget "deal" in October, 1990, much of the proposed increase in taxation revenue was scheduled to come from excise tax changes. While it may be argued that the Federal alcohol tax is in existence to discourage alcohol consumption, it is really an example of an easily enacted tax: it is relatively small on a per unit basis, and those that would protest could be easily maligned in public as supporters of alcoholism. Does a $2.14 tax on a bottle of whiskey really cause a well-to-do, pressure-ridden, alcoholic business executive to drink in moderation? Probably not.

Excise taxes are used by governments around the world. One of the most widely used excise taxes is a tax on gasoline. Most developed and industrializing countries rely heavily on imported oil and petroleum

---

EXAMPLES OF FEDERAL EXCISE TAXES
as of January 1, 1991

Alcoholic Beverages:

Whiskey, 80 proof	$2.14 per 750 ml. bottle
Beer	32 cents per six-pack
Table Wine	21 cents per bottle
Cigarettes	20 cents per pack
Gasoline	14 cents per gallon
Airline Tickets	10% of amount paid
Telephone	3% of amount paid for local and long-distance calls
Jewelry	10% on amount of price over $10,000
Automobiles	10% on amount of price over $30,000

Source: Omnibus Budget Reconciliation Act of 1990.

---

products, due to insufficient or non-existent indigenous supply sources. To minimize oil dependency, a number of countries have enacted high excise taxes on gasoline to discourage consumption, effectively doubling or tripling the final cost of the product to the consumer at the pump.

Although the United States must import over 50% of our daily oil requirement, we have continually avoided such a tax. While a Federal excise tax on gasoline does exist, it is relatively insignificant and largely unnoticed by the average consumer, and therefore does little to promote conservation. The gasoline tax at the pump was increased by 5 cents a gallon in 1990, to 14 cents. It is interesting to note that, in a time of budget incongruities, when every 1 cent increase in the gasoline tax can produce $1 billion in revenues, the gas tax in the U.S. stands at such a low level.

OPINION BUILDERS

1. *Do the current methods of taxation used by the Federal Government represent a fair and cohesive strategy for raising revenues?*

2. *Would a Federal wealth tax, perhaps imposed on some forms of property, be an appropriate addition to the taxes paid by individuals? How would such a tax affect the fairness of overall Federal taxation?*

3. *Are current personal income tax rates too high, too low, or just right?*

4. *Is the personal income tax adequately progressive?*

5. *Are corporations taxed too heavily, or do you believe that corporate income tax rates should be even higher?*

6. *Are excise taxes an appropriate mechanism for the Federal Government to employ to raise revenues?*

CHAPTER FOUR

THE EXPENDITURES OF THE FEDERAL GOVERNMENT

How to Spend One Trillion Dollars

Each February, the Office of Management and Budget puts out a summary of the President's proposed budget for the following fiscal year. It is available from the U.S. Government Printing Office to anyone who can lift it. The published budget is the size of a big-city phone book.

As one might imagine, the scope of the Federal Government is enough to justify such a large volume. The relative simplicity of the revenue side of the picture, however, is not replicated on the expenditure side - consequently the Fiscal 1992 Budget contained substantially more discussion of expenditure categories than it did of revenue sources. Yet, 2,026 pages of detail doesn't even capture every expenditure item.

The spending patterns of the Federal Government have changed over time. In the early years, Federal spending was small, in part because the nation could not afford to tax its citizens extensively. Economic prosperity changed the demands that citizens placed upon government. Public byways were needed to support commerce, national defense became a continuing, rather than episodic need, and support for the destitute emerged as a priority.

FEDERAL EXPENDITURES BY DEPARTMENT
FY 1990

Defense-Military	$289,755 M	23.1%
Treasury	255,266	20.4
Social Security	244,998	19.6
Health & Human Services	193,678	15.5
Other Independent Agencies	73,617	5.9
Agriculture	46,012	3.7
Office of Personnel Management	31,949	2.6
Veterans Affairs	28,998	2.3
Transportation	28,637	2.3
Labor	25,316	2.0
Defense-Civil	24,975	2.0
Education	23,109	1.8
Housing and Urban Development	20,167	1.6
NASA	12,429	1.0
Energy	12,014	1.0
Funds Appropriated to the President	10,087	0.8
Justice	6,507	0.5
Interior	5,796	0.5
Environmental Protection Agency	5,108	0.4
State	3,979	0.3
Commerce	3,734	0.3
Legislative Branch	2,230	0.2
The Judiciary	1,641	0.1
Small Business Administration	692	0.1
Executive Office of the President	157	0.0
General Services Administration	-123	0.0
Offsetting Receipts	-99,025	-7.9
	$1,251,703 M	

Source: Office of Management and Budget

An overwhelming percentage of today's expenditures, in fact almost 60%, is the result of only three programs - defense, Social Security, and net interest paid. The following discussion will focus on those current major categories of expenditure, and will also touch upon smaller programs when the amount and type of expenditure is of some general interest.

FEDERAL SPENDING
1990

TOTAL EXPENDITURES: $1.25 Trillion

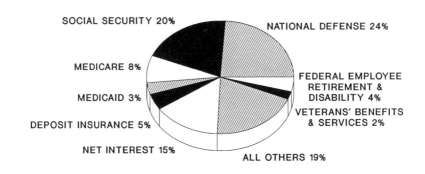

SOCIAL SECURITY 20%

MEDICARE 8%

MEDICAID 3%

DEPOSIT INSURANCE 5%

NET INTEREST 15%

NATIONAL DEFENSE 24%

FEDERAL EMPLOYEE RETIREMENT & DISABILITY 4%

VETERANS' BENEFITS & SERVICES 2%

ALL OTHERS 19%

Source: Office of Management and Budget

Defense

A significant part of the Reagan legacy is the huge military buildup of the 1980s and the burgeoning expenditures for defense. By the mid-1970s, an ever-increasing share of the budget of the Department of Defense was being used for regular expenses, such as military payrolls and the operation of existing military equipment and installations. This resulted in a squeeze on funds available for the purchase and development of new weapons. The incorporation of new technology into the operations of the military organization was slowing, jeopardizing military power in the future. Large increases in defense appropriations were granted late in the Carter Administration, and continued in the Reagan Administration, with strong advocacy from Secretary of Defense Caspar Weinberger.

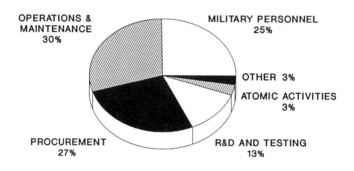

WHERE DO THE DEFENSE DOLLARS GO?
1990

TOTAL OUTLAYS: $299.3 Billion

OPERATIONS &
MAINTENANCE
30%

MILITARY PERSONNEL
25%

OTHER 3%

ATOMIC ACTIVITIES
3%

PROCUREMENT
27%

R&D AND TESTING
13%

Source: Office of Management and Budget

Partial credit for the demise of the communist regimes of Eastern Europe should be given to the U.S. military buildup during the 1980s. It is important to understand, however, the ongoing impact of that strategy on the finances of the Federal Government. Defense expenditures grew at an annual rate of 5.7% (nominal, e.g. including inflation) during the 1960s, a decade which saw the bulk of the only major military combat action this country engaged in between the Korean War and the Persian Gulf War. In the inflation-ridden 1970s, nominal defense spending increased at an annual rate of 6.1%. But in the relatively stable 1980s, the Cold War was elevated to new status, and nominal defense spending increased at an annual rate of 7.3%, to a reported $299 billion in fiscal 1990. This level of defense expenditures represents $1,197 for every man, woman, and child in the U.S. in 1990. The share of defense spending per household was approximately $3,250 in 1990 - each family worked about three and a half weeks to pay for their share of national defense.

While there has been substantial support for the limitation of defense spending over the last several years, especially after the democratization of much of the Soviet Bloc in Eastern Europe, the defense tiger may not be as easy to tame as previously thought. Not long ago, anxious members of Congress were making wish lists for the spending of what was termed the "Peace Dividend." But the invasion of Kuwait by Iraq in 1990, and the subsequent military buildup and war in the Persian Gulf serve as credible evidence to prevent any premature disarming of the American military.

ACTIVE AND RESERVE MILITARY PERSONNEL 1990

(in thousands)

	1990	1991	1992	1993
Active:	2,069	1,974	1,886	1,795
Army	751	702	660	618
Navy	583	570	551	536
Air Force	539	509	487	458
Marine Corps	197	194	188	182
Guard and Reserve:	1,128	1,176	1,068	989
Army	736	776	694	621
Navy	149	153	135	127
Air Force	198	203	199	202
Marine Corps	45	44	41	39

Note: Data for 1990 are actual. Data for 1991-1993 are estimated.
Source: Office of Management and Budget

Social Welfare Programs

The Federal Government passed the original Social Security Act in 1935. It was an important piece of the Roosevelt Administration's New Deal, and established many of the programs that exist today to improve

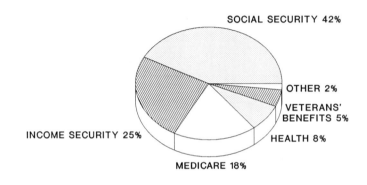

FEDERAL PAYMENTS TO INDIVIDUALS
1990

TOTAL OUTLAYS: $583.8 Billion

SOCIAL SECURITY 42%

OTHER 2%

VETERANS' BENEFITS 5%

INCOME SECURITY 25%

HEALTH 8%

MEDICARE 18%

Note: Excludes administrative costs and offsetting receipts.
Source: Office of Management and Budget

social welfare. Subsequent legislation has modified some of the original programs, and established new ones.

Today, a considerable portion of the Federal budget consists of direct payments to individuals. The major Federal social welfare programs, commonly referred to as entitlement programs, include Old Age and Survivors Insurance (Social Security), Medicare (Hospital Insurance), Disability Insurance, Medicaid, Unemployment Compensation, Food Stamps, Supplemental Security Income, veterans' benefits, and Federal employee retirement programs.

The overall level of expenditure for social welfare is certainly high, but the majority goes to support the elderly through Social Security and Medicare. For younger Americans in need, the level and breadth of benefits is usually inadequate for even basic subsistence. The average

American, who has never needed such assistance, often has a distorted perception of the generosity of social welfare programs. In reality, total spending for these programs, aside from support for the elderly, represents only a minor part of the total budget.

FEDERAL PAYMENTS TO INDIVIDUALS
1990

(Billions of Dollars)

PROGRAM CATEGORY:	DIRECT PAYMENTS	GRANTS TO STATES	TOTAL PAYMENTS
Social Security	246.5		246.5
Income Security	110.7	35.0	145.6
Medicare	107.4		107.4
Medicaid & Other Health Care	1.5	43.5	45.0
Veterans' Benefits & Services	28.4		28.4
Other	10.6	0.1	10.7
TOTALS	505.1	78.6	583.8

Note: Excludes administrative costs and offsetting receipts.
Source: Office of Management and Budget

Social Security

The largest and most significant social welfare program provided by the Federal Government is the Social Security benefit program. The primary purpose of this program is to provide pension income to those in retirement who contributed to the program during their working careers. The benefits paid are not financed by the Government's general receipts, but rather by a special tax. Regular social security benefits and administrative costs paid in fiscal year 1990 totaled $248.6 billion, or 19.9% of total Federal expenditures for that year. Chapter 9 provides a more thorough discussion of the Social Security program.

Medicare

Medicare is the second largest entitlement program sponsored by the Federal Government, and is growing very rapidly. Net expenditures for the Medicare program tripled in the 1980s, reaching $98 billion in 1990.

Medicare provides hospital insurance for the elderly and for certain other disabled persons, and most Americans aged 65 and over are eligible to participate. The regular Medicare program, Part A, is paid for by the Federal Government and does not require participants to pay a current monthly premium. Supplementary Medical Insurance, also referred to as Part B of Medicare, covers doctors' services, diagnostic tests, and other services. Part B is available for a monthly premium, which was $29.90 at the beginning of 1991. Medicare eligibility and participation is wide, as shown in the table below.

MEDICARE PARTICIPATION
Fiscal Year 1990

(in millions)

	Part A Individuals Covered	Part A Receiving Benefits	Part B Individuals Covered	Part B Receiving Benefits
Aged	30.0	6.2	29.9	24.2
Disabled	3.3	0.7	3.0	2.3
	———	———	———	———
Total	33.3	6.9	32.9	26.5

Source: Committee on Ways and Means, U.S. House of Representatives

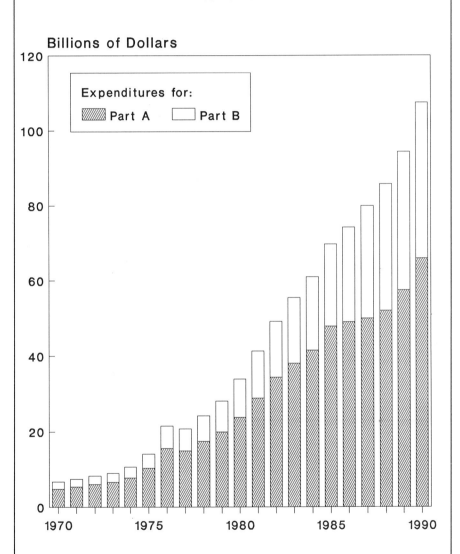

THE SKYROCKETING COST OF MEDICARE
1970-1990

Note: Includes gross outlays for payments for individuals, and excludes administrative costs and offsetting receipts.

Source: Office of Management and Budget

Medicaid

    The Medicaid program was established in 1965 to provide medical assistance to the poor and disabled. Over the years it has evolved to also include catastrophic and institutional care provisions for this group.

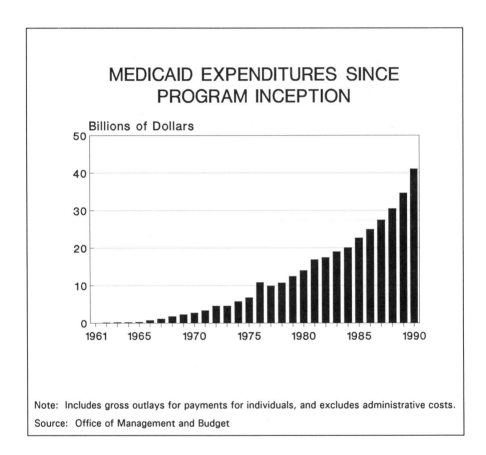

Medicaid is designed to be a joint Federal-State program. The program is administered by the individual States, following Federal guidelines, and is subsequently partially funded with Federal monies. Medicaid eligibility roughly parallels eligibility for other social welfare programs, particularly Aid to Families with Dependent Children and Supplemental Security Income. It is estimated that two-thirds of Medicaid recipients are dependent children or adults in families with dependent children. In

1990, approximately 25 million Americans received $41 billion in Medicaid benefits. Despite this hefty aid expenditure, about 25% of those at poverty level are still ineligible to receive benefits.

Income Support Programs

   With the notable exception of the support for elderly citizens, the Federal Government does not make the provision of a welfare system for the needy a top priority. Although a popular political battle cry has often been to cut domestic spending and eliminate welfare, in actuality the Federal Government spends an astonishingly small amount of its overall expenditures on social welfare programs. In fact, a complete elimination of the so-called "welfare" programs from the Federal budget would hardly make a dent in the budget deficit.

INCOME SUPPORT PROGRAMS
1990 EXPENDITURES

(in billions)

Food Stamps	$ 15.0
AFDC/Family Support	12.2
SSI	11.5
TOTAL	$38.7

For Comparison:

National Defense	$ 299.3
Interest on the National Debt	264.8
Social Security	248.6

Note: Program expenditures include benefits and administrative costs.

Source: Office of Management and Budget

The three main income support programs of the Federal Government, excluding Social Security, are Food Stamps, Supplemental Security Income (SSI), and Aid to Families with Dependent Children (AFDC). AFDC and SSI both provide cash benefits to specifically targeted low-income groups. AFDC is jointly funded by the Federal Government and the State governments, but the SSI program is funded solely by the Federal Government (although a number of states supplement SSI with state benefit payments). The Food Stamp program is financed entirely with Federal funds. The total benefits paid by the Federal Government under these three programs in 1988 was a relatively modest $32.5 billion.

PARTICIPATION IN INCOME SUPPORT PROGRAMS
(in millions)

	1975	1980	1988
Total U.S. Population	216.0	227.8	246.3
Food Stamp Recipients	16.3	19.2	18.7
as % of total population	7.5%	8.4%	7.6%
AFDC Recipients	11.1	10.6	10.9
as % of total population	5.1%	4.7%	4.4%
SSI Recipients:	3.9	3.7	4.1
as % of total population	1.8%	1.6%	1.7%

Notes: AFDC data are for fiscal year, SSI figures are for December of calendar year.
Sources: Committee on Ways and Means, U.S. House of Representatives

AFDC benefits are paid to support needy children in family situations where the earning pattern is not normal, due to the continuous absence, disability, unemployment or death of one or both parents. States are required by law to provide Medicaid to families eligible for assistance under AFDC.

SSI fills gaps left by the Social Security system. SSI is based on need, and provides income assistance for disabled and elderly citizens who are not eligible for an adequate level of Social Security benefits.

In addition to cash benefits received under AFDC or SSI, participants in those programs are generally eligible for Food Stamps.

Housing Aid

Federal housing assistance programs are operated differently than the Federal income support programs. Most notably, the Federal Government has never committed to provide housing assistance to all households and individuals who qualify for such aid. In many jurisdictions, the waiting lists for an apartment in a public housing project stretches into years. As a result, some lower income families are forced into the poorest quality housing that the private sector has to offer, or are made to spend a large amount of their total income on rent. Others are unable to make even the most modest ends meet, and become numbered among the nation's homeless.

The Federal Government provides rental assistance and mortgage interest assistance to qualifying low-income households under a variety of programs. At the beginning of FY 1990, over 5.5 million households were receiving assistance under these programs. Expenditures for housing aid in FY 1989 totaled $17.3 billion.

Interest

As the total outstanding debt of the United States Government grows, so does the amount of interest needed to pay to holders of Federal Bonds. After defense and social security spending, interest paid on the national debt is the Federal Government's third largest category of spending.

Interest is paid on a wide variety of debt obligations of the U.S. Government and its agencies. These obligations include Treasury Bills,

Treasury Notes, U.S. Savings Bonds, and many other specific securities. Total interest owed and paid on the national debt in 1990 was $265 billion. Since Federal Government trust funds with positive balances hold a large part of the national debt, the Feds paid only $184 billion in interest to public bondholders. The remaining interest was paid into the trust funds via a Government transfer, and was not considered an actual outlay. The interest burden is discussed in greater detail in Chapter 6.

Other Programs

The Resolution of Troubled Financial Institutions

The shocking and pervasive problems in the banking industry in the U.S. have captured headlines day after day. Although many banking institutions will probably come to rely on the support of Federal deposit insurance in the coming decade, the problem is stickiest in the area of savings and loan organizations.

For many years, the Federal Savings and Loan Insurance Corporation (FSLIC), an arm of the Federal Government, guaranteed individual deposits up to $100,000. Since the days of the Great Depression, agencies like the FSLIC and the Federal Deposit Insurance Corporation (FDIC) have been important stones in the foundation of nationwide confidence in the banking system. The insurance provided by these organizations substantially reduced the likelihood of frightened depositors making a "run" on their institution, fearing that if they didn't get there first, there wouldn't be any money left to pay out their holdings.

Banking deregulation of the late 1970s and early 1980s resulted in the creation of a very competitive banking market, which led to disaster. Savings and loan associations, fighting to keep depositors, raised the levels of interest they were willing to pay depositors. In some cases, these organizations then embarked upon unsound strategies and money-making schemes to ensure that ample funds would be available to pay the interest they had promised to depositors. For example, thousands of real estate projects were financed that were not economically feasible. As an additional shock, the price of oil crashed and caused an economic slump in the southwest, particularly Texas, which by some accounts is not yet over. The depressed economies in these areas led to widespread default on mortgage and loan obligations.

These practices resulted in the current multitude of savings and loan associations which do not have sufficient assets to satisfy the potential withdrawal demands of depositors. To rectify the situation, the Federal Government, in 1989, merged the remaining assets of the FSLIC into a newly-formed organization called the Resolution Trust Corporation (RTC). The RTC is responsible for eliminating the existence of insolvent S&Ls, or "thrifts", by selling off the assets to pay depositors, and making up the difference with Government funding subsidies.

Initially, the cost to the Federal Government of this exercise was estimated to be as much as $50 billion to $100 billion. However, the activities of the RTC over the last eighteen months have demonstrated that the subsidy need is probably much greater - at least $500 billion, and perhaps much more - depending on the strength of the economy and real estate market. The remedy for the insolvent S&Ls will likely be a large budget item for at least the next several years, and it will remain a particularly sharp thorn in the side of those trying to balance the finances of the Federal Government.

Foreign Aid

Foreign assistance is an area in which many Americans take a great deal of pride. It is an effort to distribute some of our bounty to those elsewhere who are less fortunate. A substantial portion of the American population today has resulted from immigration to this country in the twentieth century. Many immigrants have sought to escape harsh living conditions in their native lands, and understand how difficult it can be to survive in less affluent parts of the world.

Most Americans, however, would be astounded at the relatively meager assistance that Uncle Sam does extend abroad. Americans would be further surprised at how concentrated our foreign aid tends to be, and to which select countries it is extended.

Foreign aid is divided into several categories of assistance: military, development, and humanitarian. In many instances, the foreign aid policy of the United States is synchronized with our foreign policy. Foreign aid is frequently extended to support an important regime, and

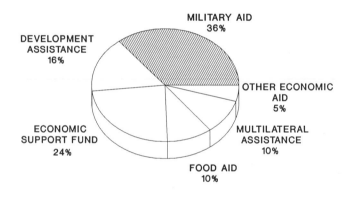

1989 U.S. FOREIGN ASSISTANCE
BY MAJOR PROGRAM

MILITARY AID
36%

DEVELOPMENT
ASSISTANCE
16%

OTHER ECONOMIC
AID
5%

ECONOMIC
SUPPORT FUND
24%

MULTILATERAL
ASSISTANCE
10%

FOOD AID
10%

Military Assistance - Grants and loans for military equipment and training provided to friendly countries.

Development Assistance - Programs which promote long term economic development.

Economic Support Fund - Economic assistance to fund balance of payments difficulties, fund imports from the U.S., or fund specific development projects.

Food Aid - Transfer of surplus American agricultural goods through direct donation or low-interest loans.

Multilateral Assistance - Contributions to multilateral development banks and economic and development programs of international organizations.

Note: Figures are estimates.
Source: Report of the Task Force on Foreign Assistance to the Committee on Foreign Affairs, U.S. House of Representatives

FOREIGN ASSISTANCE IS CONCENTRATED AMONG A FEW RECIPIENT COUNTRIES...

1989 ACTUAL OBLIGATIONS

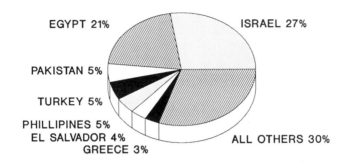

EGYPT 21%

PAKISTAN 5%

TURKEY 5%

PHILLIPINES 5%
EL SALVADOR 4%
GREECE 3%

ISRAEL 27%

ALL OTHERS 30%

THAT REMAIN BASICALLY THE SAME FROM YEAR TO YEAR

1990 ACTUAL OBLIGATIONS

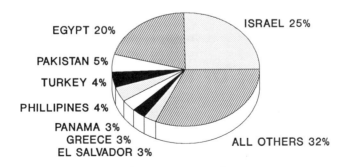

EGYPT 20%

PAKISTAN 5%

TURKEY 4%

PHILLIPINES 4%

PANAMA 3%
GREECE 3%
EL SALVADOR 3%

ISRAEL 25%

ALL OTHERS 32%

Note: Includes only country-specific aid. Expenditures for general projects, not targeted to a specific country, are not included.

Source: Agency for International Development

is less often based on real need. Aid is extended to nations that face almost imminent confrontation with a neighboring country. Consequently, much of the aid that we provide is classified as being military. Total foreign assistance provided in 1989 was approximately $15.1 billion - over 35% was of a military nature. Of the aid that was provided in 1989, almost 70% was received by only seven countries - Israel, Egypt, Pakistan, Turkey, Philippines, El Salvador, and Greece. Those same countries were the recipients of much of the country-specific aid distributed by the U.S. in 1990.

OFFICIAL DEVELOPMENT ASSISTANCE OF DEVELOPED COUNTRIES AS A PERCENT OF EACH COUNTRY'S GNP
(net disbursements)

	1986	1987	1988
AUSTRALIA	0.47	0.34	0.47
AUSTRIA	0.21	0.17	0.24
BELGIUM	0.48	0.48	0.40
CANADA	0.48	0.47	0.49
DENMARK	0.89	0.88	0.89
FINLAND	0.45	0.49	0.59
FRANCE	0.70	0.74	0.72
GERMANY	0.43	0.39	0.39
IRELAND	0.28	0.19	0.20
ITALY	0.40	0.35	0.39
JAPAN	0.29	0.31	0.32
NETHERLANDS	1.01	0.98	0.98
NEW ZEALAND	0.30	0.26	0.27
NORWAY	1.17	1.09	1.10
SWEDEN	0.85	0.88	0.87
SWITZERLAND	0.30	0.31	0.32
UNITED KINGDOM	0.31	0.28	0.32
UNITED STATES	0.23	0.20	0.21
TOTAL	0.35	0.34	0.36

Note: French figures include Overseas Departments and Territories.
Source: Organization for Economic Cooperation and Development

Arts and Humanities

Funding for the arts and humanities came under critical pressure in Congress in 1990, both as a deficit reduction target and also because of Constitutional questions of censorship. Some lawmakers proposed radical cuts in Federal spending, citing the arts as a clear example of Federal influence extending well beyond that which was intended by the

THE FEDERAL GOVERNMENT'S COMMITMENT TO THE ARTS AND HUMANITIES
(in millions)

	1989 Actual Outlays
Smithsonian Institution	$ 242.6
National Endowment for the Arts	162.2
National Endowment for the Humanities	146.3
National Gallery of Art	40.7
Historic Preservation Fund	28.1
Institute for Museum Services	22.0
John F. Kennedy Center for the Performing Arts	5.6
Commission of Fine Arts	5.5
Woodrow Wilson International Center for Scholars	4.4
Advisory Council for Historic Preservation	1.9
Total of Listed Programs	$ 659.3
Percent of Total 1989 Expenditures of the Federal Government	0.06%

FOR COMPARISON:

Grant to AMTRAK for operating losses, capital improvements, and labor protection costs	$ 574.4

Source: Office of Management and Budget

framers of the Constitution. Others in Congress supported assistance for the arts as a legitimate obligation of government, and cited examples of support for the arts given by many Western European countries.

The amount spent on arts and humanities programs sponsored by the Federal Government is difficult to tally, because definitions are imprecise and small programs are present in many different parts of the Government. Should the various performance bands of the Armed Forces be included in the funding totals? What about prison recreation programs?

In fact, the magnitude of arts and humanities spending can be ascertained by examining the major programs that are clearly cultural in orientation, such as the Smithsonian Institution and the National Endowment for the Arts. Federal spending for support of the arts and humanities constitutes less than one percent of total Federal expenditures.

Where Do We Go From Here?

When American industries were faced with tough competition from foreign suppliers in the 1980s, many responded by implementing severe cost-cutting programs. To improve efficiency, companies contracted out for services which had formerly been provided in-house, but were unrelated to their core business. In many cases, service providers outside the company proved to be less expensive than the in-house service group.

Corporate behavior in the 1980s may serve as a good model for government behavior in the 1990s. Should the Federal Government continue to provide its wide portfolio of services, or has the time come for a serious change in Government direction? The need for creative and courageous budget legislation has never been more critical.

OPINION BUILDERS

1. *Given your knowledge of the recent war in the Persian Gulf, do you believe that Federal expenditures for defense in the 1980s were too high, too low, or just right?*

2. *Considering the astonishing economic successes that America has enjoyed, do you believe that American foreign aid is too high, too low, or just right?*

3. *Should the Federal Government provide a safety net for the poor? If so, what programs should be included in that safety net, and what would be the goals and benefits of each of those programs?*

4. *Should medical care in America be provided free for all citizens, paid for by the Federal Government? If so, what taxation methods would be appropriate to pay for such a service? If not, should any sub-groups of the American citizenry be eligible for free medical care?*

5. *What is the maximum amount, in terms of percentage of total Federal expenditures, that should be used to pay interest on the Federal debt?*

CHAPTER FIVE

THE BUDGET IN HISTORICAL PERSPECTIVE

Which Economic Priorities Are In Vogue?

Over the years, as the United States grew, the size of the Federal Government expanded. Today, the importance of the role of the Federal Government in domestic affairs is unprecedented. It serves as regulator and referee of our free enterprise system, and it is responsible for the formulation and execution of economic policy in the United States.

The Evolution of Federal Economic Policy

Since the beginning of the twentieth century, economic theory has been continuously refined, thanks to the contributions of numerous economists. However, these individual contributions were often made when important pieces in the puzzle had yet to be discovered, and consequently the "fine-tuning" thought to be possible was often attempted without a full toolbox of economic adjusters. Although some are reluctant to accept it, the academic advances that have been made in the field of economic theory have not yet transformed it into an exact science.

For at least the past 60 years, economists and politicians have assumed that the Federal Government possesses marvelous powers for guiding the American economy. Although we do not have a centrally planned economic system in the communist mold, the Federal Government does exercise broad influence over the economy, usually through taxation policies and spending programs. The Government has attempted to motivate individuals to seek financial security through various tax incentives, such as allowing the deduction of mortgage interest. Tax breaks have been granted to businesses to encourage investment in new plant and equipment. The poor, elderly, and disabled have been rescued from abject poverty with Government transfer payments. Tariffs on imported products have been periodically enacted to protect the growth of a nascent industry, although the general trend in tariffs has been downward.

Despite the Government's supposed aptitude for successfully "steering" the economy, it has not been adept at keeping its books free of red ink. The ability to generate a balanced budget is a skill that few Washington politicians have mastered. In the modern political arena, the temptation to increase spending is omnipresent, while the willingness to increase taxes is generally non-existent. Annual deficits are almost certain to result from such forces, which, indeed, are frequently the outcome.

Fiscal irresponsibility, seemingly rampant in the 1980s, has not always been to blame for budget imbalances. From time to time, the Federal Government has been called upon to dramatically expand its role, so that the common good could be served.

After the laissez-faire attitude of the Federal Government toward the business community in the 1920s ended in the debacle of the Great Depression, the argument for wider Government involvement in the economy was notably advanced. The economy was in shambles - bank failures, high unemployment, and dying crops. The Great Depression demanded a reevaluation of the role of the Federal Government in the operation of the economic system.

The administration of Franklin D. Roosevelt expanded the Federal Government's role in the economy, and embraced a new economic theory which suggested that variations in government spending could be used to modulate the overall level of employment in the economy. More specifically, it was believed that higher levels of government expenditures in a recessionary environment would bring about lower levels of unemployment, and generally lead to stability and prosperity. In addition, a number of support programs were introduced as part of Roosevelt's New Deal. Senior citizens, widows, and younger survivors were given a safety net in the form of Social Security.

The Federal budget ran in deficit mode for most of the 1930s, and during the Great Depression, Federal expenditures were sometimes double the level of incoming revenues. At that time, the Government played a stabilizing role in the economy, keeping millions from becoming completely destitute.

With the incorporation of the U.S. military machine into the Allied war effort in World War II, deficit spending continued. In the mid-1940s, the U.S. Government spent amounts substantially beyond tax receipts to fight the Axis powers. In 1943, Federal spending was $78.6 billion, more than three times the $24 billion in tax revenues that were collected. Today's deficits are monstrous when considered absolutely, but on a percentage basis they do not rival the tremendous military-induced deficits incurred during World War II.

For a lengthy period following the end of World War II, a certain calm returned to the Federal budget. Lawmakers reacted to the huge debt built up during the war with an earnest fiscal conservatism. Post-war prosperity helped to keep Congress from "falling off the wagon." Social Security expenditures grew rapidly, but were accorded only minor attention because the program had been constructed to be self-financing. Other proposals to expand entitlement programs were usually defeated.

A comparison of the strength of the U.S. economy before and after World War II is staggering. Total output in 1946, measured in GNP, was almost 2.5 times what it had been in 1939. With the economy seemingly cured, Congress vowed never again to let it deteriorate as it had during the 1930s. In 1946 the Employment Act was passed, which established the pursuit of full employment as a legal and legitimate responsibility of the Federal Government, and implicitly recognized the capability the Government had for influencing the economic direction of our country.

Several budget surpluses were recorded in the late 1940s and in the 1950s. A surplus is somewhat of a political pariah, and consequently is never pursued to an extreme. The prospect of the Government socking away money at the expense of the masses is considered at best to be a "socialist plot." The budget surpluses of the post-war period were always negligible, and over time became more and more infrequent. The budget went into surplus for one last time in 1969, and then began a long and unbroken string of annual deficits.

Predicting Federal Revenues and Expenditures

Admittedly, the predicting of Federal revenues and expenditures is not a precise exercise. Tax receipts, in particular, can fluctuate unexpectedly, depending upon the overall health of the economy. If corporate profits are low, corporate income taxes collected will be low. When the unemployment rate increases, fewer workers pay their regular amount of Federal income taxes. While expenditures are more controllable, most economists agree that to continually fine tune Federal Government expenditures to match incoming receipts would only help to destabilize the economy.

For example, imagine that the Federal budget were fully in balance for a given year (revenues were expected to equal expenditures). Early in January, economic forecasters determined that corporate profits would be much lower in the January through June time period, thus expected corporate tax receipts would be $30 billion lower than previously anticipated. Corporations were also expected to lay off a sizeable number of workers, to keep from becoming unprofitable. The loss in individual income tax dollars from these layoffs was expected to be in the range of $10 billion. Now the budget is unlikely to be in balance, because $40 billion of anticipated receipts have been lost. If the Federal Government were then to reduce Federal wages by $40 billion to keep its budget in balance, even more income tax dollars would be lost from the declining wage base of Federal workers. As fewer people held regular jobs, personal spending would become more conservative, causing stores to sell less and order less from manufacturers, and the "multiplier" effect could be much more severe than it would have been if the Government had simply accepted a budget deficit for the year. A stable stream of

Government spending, because it is such a large and important part of the economy, helps the economic system remain on sound footing, and keeps it from slipping into a recessionary death spiral.

In many ways expenditures are much easier than revenues for the Federal Government to predict. Most Federal agencies and departments are able to control spending within an approved budget. A large portion of expenditures represent programs and fundings which are planned several years in advance. Many of the entitlement programs existing today have complex forecasting models which predict the number of beneficiaries expected in the future, along with the likely level of inflation and cost of living increases that beneficiaries will need. The Social Security Administration, for example, has several financial scenarios which look into the future, forecasting tax contributions and paid benefits from the Old Age and Survivors Insurance Trust Fund well into the middle of the next century. Military hardware development and procurement is another example of Federal spending which has a long planning horizon.

Supply-Side Economics

Small deficits, even when they recur year after year, have generally not drawn major criticism from the community of economists. Some say that a deficit equal to 1% of GNP is acceptable on an annual basis. In the course of managing the economy and working toward full employment (minimizing unemployment), which you will recall is a legal responsibility of the Federal Government, budget deficits are likely to occur. The financing of a budget deficit is usually accomplished easily, simply by having the Treasury sell bonds. Since World War II, the Federal budget has been in surplus only eight times. Deficits have generally been the rule rather than the exception, and have come in all shapes and sizes.

The Federal financing situation began to deteriorate in the late 1970s. By the time the Carter Administration left office in early 1981, the Federal Government was well on its way to posting its largest budget deficit ever: $73.8 billion. By today's standards, that amount seems almost immaterial. But at the time, it caused great concern both to the incoming Reagan Administration and to those on Capitol Hill.

The level of inflation in the U.S. economy picked up steam in the late 1970s, pushing up expenditures dramatically in a wide range of Government programs. At the same time, tax receipts were also increasing, as salary inflation pushed more and more people into higher tax brackets. In the end, however, tax receipts were unable to keep pace with the level of expenditure, after falling behind in the "stagflation" period of the mid-1970s.

The current deficit problem can be traced to the beginning of the Reagan presidency. The "supply-side" economic theory embraced by the Reagan Administration was centered around making "big government" much smaller. Reagan's economic team called for tax cuts and special tax provisions, for both individuals and businesses, to stimulate the economy, and also sought an overall reduction in the size of the Federal Government.

The supply-side economic theory, in its most rudimentary form, states that a smaller tax burden on individuals and businesses increases economic incentives, as well as spending, and thereby leads to a greater amount of entrepreneurial activity and additional growth. As the economy grows, the increase in taxable incomes generated by new employment and increased profits flows back into the government's coffers, and more than offsets the impact of the previous tax cut.

In a flurry of conservative demagoguery, and a presumed "mandate for change," David Stockman, Chief of the Office of Management and Budget, and President Reagan pushed the Economic Recovery Tax Act of 1981 through the Congress. The law restructured the individual income tax, bringing about a 25% reduction in rates over three years. The tax break was the centerpiece of the supply side economics program, and was to be accompanied by large reductions in Federal expenditures.

Unfortunately, the fiscal balance sought by the Reagan group never materialized. The budget balance was permanently derailed by two crucial miscalculations: 1) that Federal spending could be reduced,

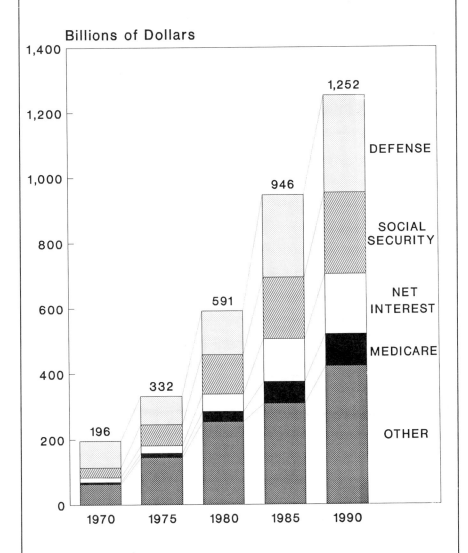

EXPENDITURES CONTINUE TO RISE
MAJOR FEDERAL SPENDING CATEGORIES

Source: Office of Management and Budget

and 2) that inflation would continue at a moderately high rate. Neither of these conditions came to pass.

Soon after persuading the Congress to embrace his tax cut proposal, Reagan began the arduous task of finding the necessary budget cuts to make his whole package work. The reluctance of Congress to pass the tax reduction measure was only surpassed by its unwillingness to push through the necessary budget cuts to balance the budget after agreeing to lower taxes. Protracted battles were fought to reduce Government spending, but the extraordinary revenue loss caused by the tax cut could not be matched by expense reductions. In the end, he and his team were unsuccessful, in part because they had been unrealistic from the outset. The defense capability was in need of some modernization, and substantial growth in defense spending was approved. Further, cuts elsewhere in the budget were difficult to achieve, due both to special interest groups and the reluctance of legislators to reduce or eliminate ongoing program expenditures.

In addition, the level of inflation dropped off dramatically after the tax cut, due to restrictive money supply growth resulting from policies being pursued by the Federal Reserve. It had been expected that the overall revenue impact of the tax cut, which was to be spread over three years, would be minimal. The program granted a 25% reduction in tax rates, with a first year cut of 5%, followed by two successive yearly cuts of 10%. Beginning in 1985, the income tax brackets were to be indexed for inflation. In the meantime, the level of inflation during the phase-in period was anticipated to dampen the effect that the tax cut might otherwise have on the revenue coffers. But the sharp decrease in inflation that followed caused the 1981 tax act to permanently reduce the tax burden on individuals.

An endless string of increasing budget deficits began, their sizes unprecedented by all measures, in peace-time America. By fiscal year 1983, the deficit had climbed to $207.8 billion, and by 1985 had grown to $212.3 billion. The President and Congress searched for politically palatable solutions to the problem. Some legislators sought a balanced budget amendment to the Constitution, while others looked to provide the President with the power of a line-item veto in the budget. The line item

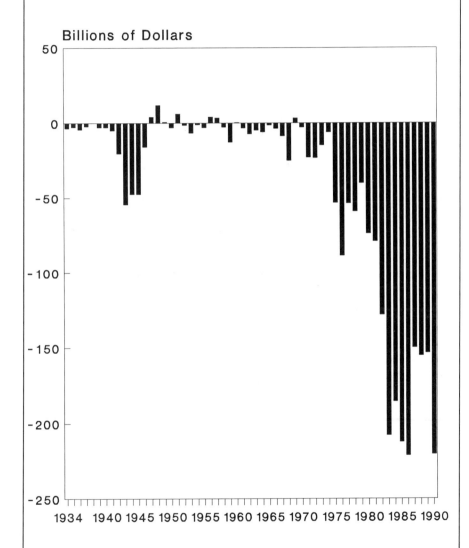

SURPLUSES AND DEFICITS SINCE 1934
THE IMBALANCE OF THE FEDERAL BUDGET

Note: Figures for 1976 include the Transition Quarter (TQ), representing 5 fiscal quarters.

Source: Office of Management and Budget

veto would allow the President to reject individual budget items without derailing the passage of the comprehensive budget package.

The inability to correct the imbalance has resulted in the mortgaging of America's future. It has allowed many of the fortunes made in the prosperous 1980s to go largely untaxed, those revenue opportunities lost forever.

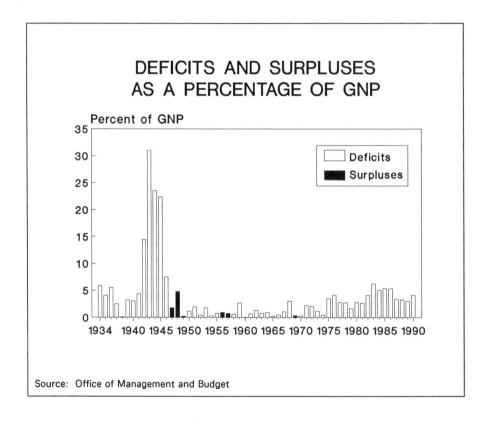

Fixing the Budget

Congress traditionally has had a very difficult time adjusting for imbalances between spending and revenues. Our legislators are never enthusiastic about raising taxes - it doesn't play well at the polls. Equally unpopular are spending cuts, particularly when they result in the closing of some Federal installation in a particular Congress member's jurisdiction. To try to adjust for these inclinations given the looming budget imbalances, Congress in 1985 passed the Balanced Budget and Emergency Deficit Control Act, more popularly known as Gramm-Rudman-Hollings, or Gramm-Rudman. This legislation set specific deficit targets, which declined to zero over several years. The failure to meet such targets, either by adjusting outlays downward or receipts upward, was supposed to result in mandatory spending cuts administered across the board (although all departments were not to be affected at an equal rate).

Unfortunately, procedural loopholes reduced the effectiveness of the deficit reduction legislation. Optimistic projections for economic growth and Government tax receipts, sanctioned by Government officials, were used to project Federal deficits which fell within the parameters of Gramm-Rudman. When these projections were not met, Gramm-Rudman failed completely in its attempt to take a bite out of the deficit. In fact, the deficit has grown since the original Gramm-Rudman legislation was passed, and subsequent legislative adjustments to the 1985 bill have only served to delay the day of final budget reckoning.

In 1990, the Federal budget deficit was $220 billion, or 4.1% of GNP. If the $36 billion surplus in Social Security is left out of the calculation, along with several other items considered to be "off-budget", the 1990 deficit is more accurately represented as $277 billion, or 5.1% of GNP. These numbers should be enough to cause insomnia for every American. Unfortunately, 1990 is not an isolated year with respect to the size of the annual deficit. Since 1982, the budget deficit on an annual basis has exceeded 3% of GNP, even when the annual Social Security surplus benefits the calculation.

OPINION BUILDERS

1. Is it acceptable, and perhaps necessary, to have the Federal Government operate in deficit mode year after year?

2. *Would it be inappropriate for the Federal Government to run a budget surplus year after year if it were used to pay down the Federal debt? Would such a series of continuing surpluses represent overtaxation?*

3. *Given the relatively large budget deficits in recent years, in conjunction with relatively low Federal income tax rates, is it conceivable that some taxpayers have had an unusually light Federal tax burden?*

CHAPTER SIX

THE ACCUMULATED FEDERAL DEBT

The Debt That Keeps On Taking

When discussing the budget for the Federal Government's operations, it is important to separate the concept of the *annual* budget deficit from the concept of the total *accumulated* Federal debt. Each year, the Government plans to offset expenditures by expected receipts. If receipts fail to meet the level of money expended, this results in a budget deficit. Conversely, if receipts exceed actual expenses, the result is a budget surplus. These annual surpluses and deficits build on each other and, because the annual budget is more frequently in deficit than surplus, the result is the total accumulated Federal debt.

Early in this country's history, the Federal Government was confronted with the problem of money that had been spent by the Revolutionary Army, but had not been collected through taxes. The new government of George Washington assumed these obligations, and launched the United States on a path of credit spending.

Since that time, the Government's ability to spend on credit has risen to a nearly professional level. Sums of money large enough to startle even a banker are regularly spent without revenue to compensate for such expenditure.

Just as an individual using a credit card must have authority to carry a certain credit balance from one month to the next, so must the Federal Government have authority to carry a given level of accumulated debt. The Federal Government's "credit limit" is established by our proxy body for popular opinion, Congress. An individual's credit card has a credit limit, and the Federal Government has a debt ceiling. The debt ceiling is adjusted periodically by an act of Congress, which must be approved by the President (or must be approved by such a majority of Congress that an override of a Presidential veto is possible).

While the debt ceiling may appear to be an actual barrier and prohibit overspending by the Government, in fact it is not much more than a regularly updated approximation of the total outstanding Federal debt. The Federal debt ceiling has been raised over 50 times since 1950, and stood at $4.1 trillion at the end of December, 1990. A failure to raise the debt ceiling in a period of high expenditures and low receipts, when deficit spending was a certainty, would result in the shutdown of most Federal Government activities.

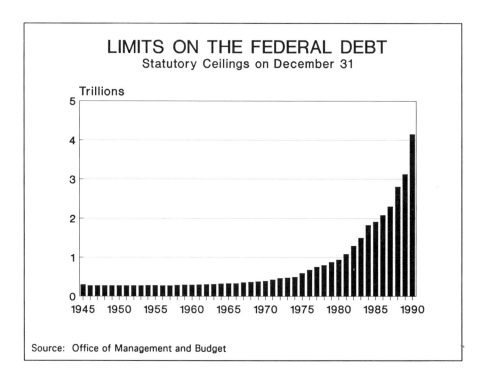

LIMITS ON THE FEDERAL DEBT
Statutory Ceilings on December 31

Source: Office of Management and Budget

From an economic perspective, carrying forward a debt balance is not always inadvisable. The important chalk line is drawn between prudence and over-indulgence. The assumption of a relatively modest amount of long term debt, in a period where Government revenues are low, can serve to encourage growth, if the money is expended properly. On the other hand, a large deficit or a burdensome level of debt can begin to constrict the ability of Congress to respond to recessionary pressures with stimulative economic policies. Demand for new Treasury Bond issues is likely to be minimal if the financial marketplace has already been flooded with previous Treasury securities. In such a scenario, new debt money may become difficult to find. Furthermore, the need to set aside several hundred billion dollars each year just to pay interest means that Congress has that much less to use to fund more tangible and beneficial programs.

Home ownership entails a debt commitment with which many Americans are familiar. A home mortgage, typically granted for a thirty year time horizon, is a good example of the effective employment of long term debt. Assuming a modest amount of inflation each year of 4% with matching cost-of-living adjustments to salaries, an individual who earns $20,000 in year 1 would be earning almost $65,000 in Year 30. A home purchased for $35,000 in Year 1, with 10% down and a 30 year, fixed rate mortgage carrying an interest rate of 10%, would cost approximately $3,300 per year in principal and interest payments. With a fixed rate mortgage, this obligation would remain constant in each of the thirty years over the life of the loan. In Year 1, principal and interest would consume 16.5% of the $20,000 gross salary, but in Year 30 would be only 5.1% of the $65,000 gross salary. In the meantime, the mere advance of salary by 4% per year may not have changed the standard of living of the receiving individual by much over the thirty years, because price inflation was matching salary increases. Clearly, the burden of housing cost has become much less significant.

To this date, the U.S. has been unable to completely eradicate inflation from its economy. It is reasonable to assume that, at the very least, some small level of inflation will continue to exist. The existence of such inflation can serve the Federal debt burden as it serves the 30 year mortgage holder. Debt accrued today can be paid off in cheaper dollars many years from now.

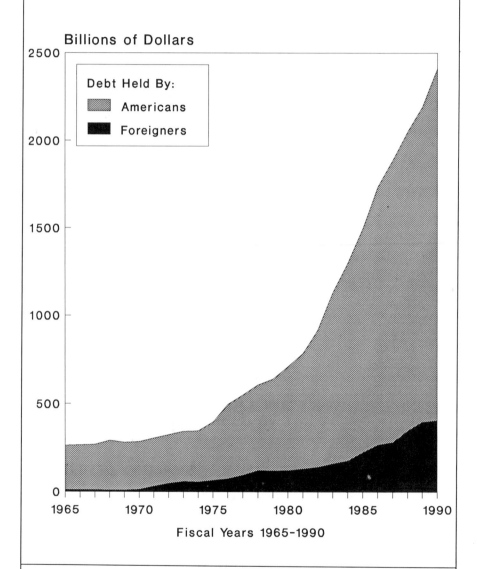

HOW MUCH DO WE OWE?
FEDERAL DEBT HELD BY THE PUBLIC

Note: Excludes agency debt, the holdings of which are believed to be small. Debt held by foreign entities and individuals are estimates provided by the Treasury Department.

Source: Office of Management and Budget

The Federal budget deficit for fiscal 1990 was $220 billion. At this level, to have balanced the budget for one year through increased income taxes would have required an additional $2,400 from each American household.

Another interesting statistic is derived from the total accumulated Federal debt. On December 31, 1990, that debt stood at $3,365 billion, a sum incomprehensible for most people. The total sales of the Fortune 500 for 1989 were only $2,600 billion, 23% less than the accumulated Federal debt. More dramatically, for every U.S. citizen, there are $13,350 in Federal debt obligations.

The total outstanding Federal debt grew at an unprecedented rate in the 1980s. In 1980, the Federal debt stood at $908 billion, or $4,010 for every citizen. Between 1980 and 1990, the total Federal debt grew at an annual rate of 14%.

Such a large amount of debt is staggering, and the cost of carrying that debt is particularly alarming. In 1990, net interest paid on the Federal debt was $184.2 billion, or 14.7% of the total expenditures of the Federal Government. Once again, this interest expense represented $736 per citizen. Since 1980, the Federal Government has paid almost $1.3 trillion in interest.

The Reagan Administration, in conjunction with the Congress, cut Federal income taxes by 25% in 1981 through the passage of the Economic Recovery Tax Act. Considering today's situation, an interesting parallel can be imagined. Assume first that in 1990 the Federal budget had been in balance: revenues were able to offset all of expenditures. If some organization, perhaps the Foundation for Debt Burden Eradication, were then to donate enough money to pay off the accumulated Federal debt in its entirety, a tax cut could be made possible. In such a situation, the current administration would be able to grant another tax cut of nearly 15% simply through the savings on interest payments, which would vanish along with the disappearing accumulated debt.

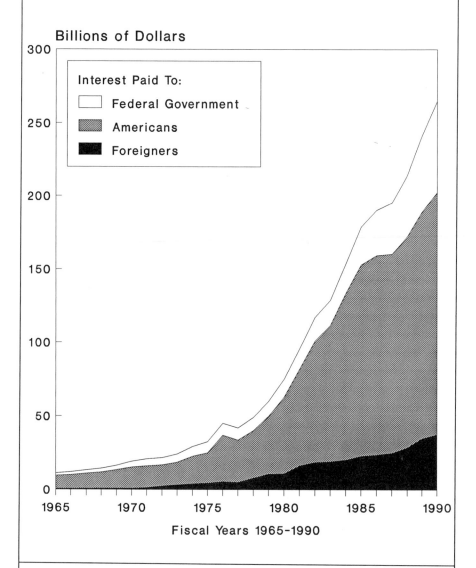

HOW MUCH INTEREST DO WE PAY?
INTEREST PAID BY THE FEDERAL GOVERNMENT

Billions of Dollars

Interest Paid To:

Federal Government

Americans

Foreigners

Fiscal Years 1965-1990

Note: Interest paid to non-government entities and individuals are estimates provided in the FY 1992 Budget. Figures for 1976 include the Transition Quarter, July-September 1976.

Source: Office of Management and Budget

Merely eliminating the budget deficit will have little impact on the ongoing burden of interest. Until the amount of debt outstanding is reduced, the burden of interest will change very little. Since the prospect of a mythical foundation rescuing the Government with a donation is very small, the only way to reduce the total debt is to pay it down through a series of budget surpluses.

OPINION BUILDERS

1. *Does the current level of the accumulated Federal debt represent a burden on future generations of Americans?*

2. *Should the Federal Government be required to balance the Federal budget each and every year?*

3. *Should the President have the power to veto any item in the Federal budget after it has been approved by Congress, or should the President be required to either accept or reject the Congressionally-approved budget in total?*

CHAPTER SEVEN

GRAMM-RUDMAN AND THE DEFICIT
REDUCTION MOVEMENT

Trying to Tame the Budget Tiger

The huge deficits run by the Federal Government in the early 1980s sent a chill across Capitol Hill. Most politicians knew that they had gotten themselves into a severe situation. Taxes had been cut without first having a blueprint for expense reductions, and the financial condition of the Federal Government had been steadily eroding.

In desperation, Congress passed a law that was intended to redirect the budget toward sound financial ground. The Balanced Budget and Emergency Deficit Control Act of 1985 was approved by Congress to provide a policing mechanism against the temptation to further increase spending without adding new revenues. In one respect, it was a cowardly piece of legislation - if members of Congress had really wanted to reduce the deficit, they would have simply raised taxes or cut expenditures. But, fearful of facing a reprisal at the voting precincts, few were willing to take the more direct route.

On December 12, 1985, the Balanced Budget and Emergency Deficit Control Act became law. It was jointly sponsored by Senator Phil Gramm of Texas (R), Senator Warren Rudman of New Hampshire (R), and Senator Ernest Hollings of South Carolina (D).

The purpose of the Gramm-Rudman legislation was to force the Government to confront the deficit issue. The budget deficit had taken on an annually renewable life of its own, and it was not predicted to diminish over time. The law did not seek an unrealistic and unachievable immediate solution to the problem; rather, it legislated the gradual elimination of the deficit problem. The ultimate goal of the Gramm-Rudman initiative was a balanced budget in fiscal year 1990. That was a goal that was not achieved.

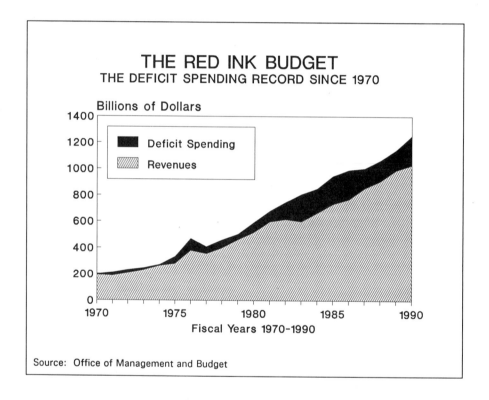

THE RED INK BUDGET
THE DEFICIT SPENDING RECORD SINCE 1970

Billions of Dollars

Legend:
■ Deficit Spending
▨ Revenues

Fiscal Years 1970-1990

Source: Office of Management and Budget

While Gramm-Rudman sought a balanced *annual* budget, its mandated goal was probably not a balanced budget in the simplest sense. First, it did not address the *accumulated* Federal debt at all. The interest burden on that debt was to continue to exert major pressure each year. Second, for the purpose of measuring compliance with the deficit targets, activities in the Social Security trust funds were co-mingled with the main part of the Federal budget. This co-mingling turned out to be a major shortcoming of the original Gramm-Rudman legislation.

After the 1982 amendments to the Social Security Act, the Social Security trust funds began to generate substantial surpluses each year. The Social Security tax had been modified and increased, so that a reserve balance could be built in anticipation of the expected large population of retirees in the middle of the 21st century. Under Gramm-Rudman, the sizable surpluses accruing each year in the Federal Old Age and Survivors Insurance Trust Fund (Social Security) and the Federal Disability Insurance Trust Fund were to be included in the overall deficit calculation, distorting the real deficit picture. In fact, without the large excess cashflow from the Social Security system, Congress would have faced a series of fiscal problems in the 1980s that would have been cause for serious concern.

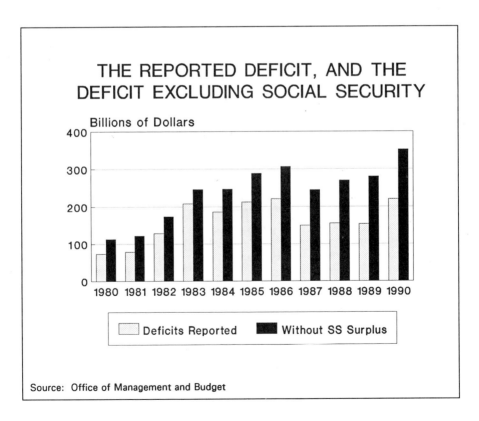

THE REPORTED DEFICIT, AND THE DEFICIT EXCLUDING SOCIAL SECURITY

Billions of Dollars

Deficits Reported   Without SS Surplus

Source: Office of Management and Budget

A TALE OF UNACHIEVED GOALS
($ billions)

	1985 TARGETS	1987 TARGETS	1990 TARGETS	ACTUAL DEFICIT
1986	171.9			221.2
1987	144.0			149.7
1988	108.0	144.0		155.1
1989	72.0	136.0		153.4
1990	36.0	100.0		220.4
1991	0	64.0	327.0	
1992		28.0	317.0	
1993		0	236.0	
1994			102.0	
1995			83.0	

Note: Targets established in 1990 exclude surpluses from the Social Security trust funds, and consequently show a more accurate picture of the size of the underlying deficit.

Sources: Balanced Budget and Emergency Deficit Control Act of 1985, Balanced Budget and Emergency Deficit Control Reaffirmation Act of 1987, Omnibus Budget Reconciliation Act of 1990.

The original language of Gramm-Rudman contained an enforcement mechanism. Prior to the October 1 start of a fiscal year, the Congressional Budget Office (CBO) and the Office of Management and Budget (OMB) were to jointly determine if the projected deficit for the upcoming fiscal year exceeded the deficit target by more than $10 billion. If the deficit target was expected to be missed by greater than $10 billion, then automatic cutbacks were to occur on October 15, with 50% of the excess deficit taken out of the defense budget, and 50% taken out of "non-defense programs" (a number of non-defense programs were exempt from any cutback, including Social Security, some veterans' benefits, and a number of entitlement, credit, and insurance programs).

One of the most important shortcomings of the Gramm-Rudman legislation was the fact that its remedies were based on projected revenues and expenditures, rather than actual numbers. No retrospective actions were mandated. If the deficit was estimated to be $30 billion at the start of a fiscal year, and that was within the established deficit target range, then no automatic cutbacks would occur, even if the actual deficit turned out to exceed the $30 billion by a substantial margin. The legislation did not require the Government to "make-up" any excess deficit from the previous year. Once a deficit was recorded, it became a permanent part of the total Federal debt.

By 1987, the Federal Government had fallen far behind the ambitious goals of the original Gramm-Rudman law. The Balanced Budget and Emergency Deficit Control Reaffirmation Act of 1987 established new deficit targets, and extended the time horizon of the original legislation. The new target for the balanced budget was set at fiscal year 1992.

Getting the CBO and the OMB to agree on a set of economic projections had proven to be difficult. In the revised law, CBO was charged with the responsibility of providing estimates of the upcoming deficit to OMB, but final authority for forecasting the deficit and activating the sequestration process was given to OMB (interestingly, OMB deficit projections are usually much more optimistic than those of CBO).

The 1987 revisions to Gramm-Rudman did not include any correction to the loophole that allowed actual deficits which exceeded projected deficits. The law remained devoid of any real accountability. If a deficit actually came in above the target and the previous estimate, it was simply a point in history, in no need of redress.

In 1990, the budget process broke down entirely. The revised deficit targets had been repeatedly missed, and Democrats and Republicans were at odds over what would be the best approach to take going forward. For weeks on end, Washington stood ready to witness the shutdown of the Federal Government for lack of an adopted budget to authorize spending and receipts for fiscal year 1991, which began on October 1, 1990. Finally, after an exceedingly painful public display of partisan politics, the White House and Congress agreed to the 1991 budget.

BUDGET DEFICIT PROJECTIONS CHANGE FREQUENTLY

	1991	1992	1993	1994	1995
OMB & President: FY 91 Budget	63	25	+6	+11	+9
CBO: October 1990	253	262	170	56	29
OMB & President: FY 92 Budget	318	281	202	62	3
CBO: January 1991	298	284	215	160	57

Note: All projections are estimates. OMB figures represent expected deficit and surplus levels assuming the enactment of proposed budget changes. CBO projections are based on current law, and assume that discretionary caps established during the budget summit in 1990 will be followed. All figures include surpluses projected for Social Security and other off-budget categories.

Sources: Office of Management and Budget and Congressional Budget Office

---

OPINION BUILDERS

1.   Was the Gramm-Rudman-Hollings law an adequate attempt to reign in Federal spending?

2.   Should deficit targets be strictly or loosely interpreted and enforced?

3. *How frequently should Federal spending be adjusted to conform to deficit targets, assuming that changes in the economic climate are inevitable?*

CHAPTER EIGHT

THE BUDGET AGREEMENT OF 1990

Bipartisan Brinksmanship

Although Congress had passed two separate deficit reduction bills, one in 1985 and one in 1987, the budget imbalance persisted. Year after year, the deficit dragon continued to rear its ugly head. The Gramm-Rudman-Hollings laws simply were not airtight enough to maintain the course toward a balanced budget.

The budget for fiscal year 1991, which runs from October 1, 1990 through September 30, 1991, was submitted to Congress by President Bush and his advisors in late January of 1990. It was packed with White House prescriptions for tax policy changes and spending limitations. When the columns were tallied, the budget proposal projected a 1991 deficit of $64 billion, meeting the established Gramm-Rudman-Hollings target. Looking forward, the budget also proposed a series of revenue and expenditure streams that would put the budget in balance by 1993.

The delivery of the budget book marked the official beginning of the 1990 budget battle. It might as well have been launched in a missile, fired from the White House, down Pennsylvania Avenue, aimed at the Capitol Dome. Although the war of rhetoric was just beginning, the battle lines had actually been drawn long before the budget book appeared on the Capitol Hill best-seller list.

In some ways, this budget battle was inevitable. After years of fiscal gerrymandering, the electorate was fed up. There was loud public opposition to both tax increases and spending cuts. Satisfying both camps was impossible, even if the status quo were maintained. The buildup of military strength in the Persian Gulf made defense cuts unlikely in the near term, and the lobbying power of the elderly and retired continued to make it extremely difficult to propose any changes in Social Security or Medicare, the two largest domestic programs.

Some members of Congress remembered the Reagan tax cut bitterly, and hoped that once and for all the Federal tax revenue stream could be put back on track. These legislators were prepared to take President Bush to the mat on his "no new taxes" pledge, and they savored the opportunity to increase the rate of taxation on the rich, a policy shift that they knew would play very well at the middle class voting precincts. Democrats anxiously anticipated the riding of populist sentiment to victory over their Republican nemeses at the polls in November.

The collapse of communism in Eastern Europe at the end of 1989, and the alleged end to the Cold War raised some interesting possibilities. A number of elected officials on Capitol Hill anxiously looked forward to the soon-to-be-diminishing defense budget, and the opportunities it would bring for balancing the overall Federal budget and increasing spending in domestic social programs, such as child care, education, and health care. These legislators saw their political fortunes in the "Peace Dividend," much as legislators had looked hopefully to the expected "Vietnam Dividend" in the late 1960s. More than a few members of Congress thought privately about directing some of the expected bounty into their own districts, with hopes of cementing their own grassroots support.

Ultimately, all concerned had taken an extremely optimistic view of the coming budget extravaganza. Congress seemed to have an almost religious belief that somehow Gramm-Rudman would save them. And the Bush proposals identified a continuing pattern of correction from the deficit high of $221 billion in 1986. In actuality, the second largest deficit spending year to date would turn out to be 1990, and the evidence would soon surface that there was really no continuing deficit correction at all, but that the deficit was spiraling further out of control.

Budget maneuvering continued through the spring and the summer of 1990, but no agreement between the Congress and the White House could be reached. Bush continued to trumpet his pledge not to raise taxes, making it more and more politically difficult for him to later back away from the promise. With each reiteration of that vow, opponents in Congress dug in their heels and became more entrenched in their dissention. The President also kept up his quest for a reduction in the tax rate on long-term capital gains, which had been part of his original 1991 budget proposal. The capital gains tax issue became another headache for Congress, an initiative even some Republicans did not support.

The budget negotiations became more urgent as the summer dragged on, and the gulf between the White House and the Capitol did not narrow. Official Federal spending authority expires each September 30 if a new budget is not approved. As September 30, 1990 approached, a shut-down of the Federal Government's operations became a distinct possibility.

On September 7, the budget talks between the White House policymakers and Congressional leaders moved from the Capitol to Andrews Air Force Base in suburban Maryland, not far from downtown Washington. For ten days, negotiators tried to reach an agreement at their "budget retreat," seeking a budget proposal that could survive bipartisan scrutiny on Capitol Hill and eventually be rewarded with the signature of the President. But no budget deal was struck at Andrews.

Negotiations continued as the September 30 deadline approached. An agreement was reached on September 30, but it was summarily defeated in Congress.

The next several weeks were harrowing and embarrassing for Washington lawmakers. The ongoing financial viability of the Federal Government was continually brought into question. A series of several stopgap spending authorizations were passed, allowing the Government to continue operating. At one point, however, deadlocked without a funding authorization for a weekend, the Government did cease operations for three days. Disappointed tourists visiting Washington found monuments and museums closed.

THE IMPACT OF THE 1990 BUDGET AGREEMENT

REVENUE ENHANCEMENTS

INCOME TAX CHANGES	Changes top marginal tax rate to 31%, introduces a phase-out of personal exemptions and a reduction in allowable deductions for higher income taxpayers.	$ 40 B
MEDICARE PAYROLL TAX	Increase the cap on wages subject to the 1.45% payroll tax to $125,000.	27
GASOLINE TAX	Increase the gasoline tax by 5 cents per gallon.	25
EXCISE TAXES	Raise excise taxes on tobacco, alcohol, airline tickets, and gas-guzzling cars. Extend tax on telephone usage. Impose new taxes on certain luxury goods, including expensive cars, furs, and jewelry.	41
SOCIAL SECURITY	Extend to all state and local government employees not covered by a government-sponsored pension plan.	9
INSURANCE COMPANY TAXES	Limit tax deductions for property and casualty and life insurers.	9
OTHER TAXES	Small, miscellaneous tax increases and decreases, and collection enhancements.	7

SPENDING CUTS

MEDICARE	Lower reimbursements to doctors and hospitals, and higher premiums and deductibles for participants.	$ 43 B
FEDERAL PENSIONS	Eliminate lump-sum payment option for most Federal retirees; other retirement and health benefits savings.	14
FARM SUBSIDIES	Lower farm price support payments.	12
BANK FEES	Increase deposit insurance premiums.	9
DEFENSE	Reduction in outlays, with more to come.	91
INTEREST	Lower expected debt service costs.	45

NEW SPENDING		
EARNED INCOME TAX CREDIT	Increase to offset effects of new taxes, and to help pay for child care and health insurance.	$-17 B
OTHER	Increases in non-defense discretionary spending.	-26
SPENDING CUTS TO BE MADE		
DISCRETIONARY SPENDING	Spending cuts, mostly in defense, remaining to be made in order to meet overall reduction goal.	$ 149 B
INTEREST	Additional expected debt service savings.	16
TOTAL IMPACT ON FEDERAL DEFICIT OVER 5 YEARS		**$ 496 Billion**
Source: Congressional Budget Office		

After modifications to the earlier agreement, the Omnibus Budget Reconciliation Act of 1990 was passed by Congress on the weekend of October 27-28. It was comprised of tax increases, cuts in program expenditures, and changes in the way the budget would be enforced. The new law emphasized spending control, rather than the traditional deficit reduction focus mandated by Gramm-Rudman. The agreement contained three major budget guidelines: spending caps on discretionary programs, a "pay-as-you-go" rule for mandatory revenue and expenditure programs, and adjustable deficit targets.

The Feds distinguish between discretionary and mandatory spending. Discretionary spending must be authorized on an annual basis. Revenues and expenditures for mandatory programs, such as entitlements (e.g. Medicare), are continued automatically from year to year. No annual action is required of Congress to maintain the programs.

The budget agreement established annual spending caps for military, domestic, and international discretionary spending, covering the 1991-1993 time period. If spending in any category exceeds the cap, an automatic spending cut will be levied against each program in that category. In addition, total discretionary appropriations were subject to caps in 1994 and 1995.

Mandatory programs will be policed under the new law. Programs may be altered, but the total effect on the budget of all modifications to mandatory items must net to zero. Legislated changes which increase mandatory expenditures or reduce tax receipts are to be offset by compensating adjustments - this is the "pay-as-you-go" requirement.

Finally, to take some of the crystal ball mystique out of the deficit reduction process, the budget agreement established new, adjustable deficit targets. The legislation revised the old deficit targets, which, much like earlier established targets, had also been missed. The new targets reflect the removal of the Social Security surpluses from the deficit calculation.

While this appealed to budget analysts, in reality, the deficit target concept was weakened considerably in the new legislation. Under the new law, the President can revise the deficit targets when presenting the 1992-1995 budgets to Congress, allowing adjustments for "economic realities." In addition, the President can declare spending for a national emergency to be exempt from the spending limits.

The budget legislation is expected to reduce the budget deficits in the 1991-1995 time frame by approximately $496 billion in total, falling slightly short of the $500 billion reduction that had been sought. It is, however, far from being a certainty. The Congressional Budget Office expressed some skepticism in a report issued in December of 1990, cautioning that almost $150 billion in discretionary spending cuts over the five year period have yet to be identified. And as is repeatedly demonstrated on the Hill, consensus on issues requiring thriftiness is difficult to attain.

Despite all of the maneuvering, the law is unlikely to result in the elimination of the deficit. The adjustable deficit reduction targets forged by the budget agreement are inherently weak. In fact, the Congressional Budget Office reported that the annual deficit in 1995 would still represent 0.4 percent of GNP, even if the discretionary spending caps prove to be effective, and the deficit problem may linger on even longer. The further deterioration in the economy after the passage of the budget legislation is projected to have an effect on tax revenues collected, and will continue upward pressure on the annual deficits over the next few years.

Once again, it appears that our elected officials have made much ado about nothing. The opportunity to remake the role of the Federal Government in American society has been missed. The quick and superficial fixes mandated by the 1990 budget legislation are, in some cases, laughable. Rather than reevaluate the fairness of the income tax system, and examine it carefully for additional revenue opportunities, there will be new taxes on luxury goods. Instead of scrutinizing the real financial need of some elderly Medicare beneficiaries, an extension of the Medicare payroll tax for younger citizens was approved. In general, expensive programs and policies have been allowed to remain in place, with no credible means established for covering the funding shortfall.

OPINION BUILDERS

1. *Was the long debate surrounding the 1991 Federal budget evidence that the budget approval process is in need of serious renovation, or was it simply a result of difficult financial conditions?*

2. *How might the budget process be reformed?*

3. *Should Members of Congress be subject to limitations on the number of years that they are eligible to serve? If so, what should those limitations be?*

4. *Do you believe that a Congress consisting entirely of newly-elected, freshmen members would be better or worse at solving problems than our current, incumbency-oriented legislature?*

CHAPTER NINE

THE SOCIAL SECURITY TRUST FUNDS

A Surprising Surplus

Social Security is the largest entitlement program sponsored by the Federal Government. This program pays out a staggering amount of cash benefits each year, primarily to elderly and retired citizens. But even with such large annual obligations, part of the attractiveness of the Social Security program is that it is self-funding.

The benefits provided through the Social Security program arose out of the desire to protect elderly and certain other individuals from poverty, when they became unable to provide for themselves any longer. Through the years, Social Security has grown in importance, and has become almost a protected right in the minds of many Americans. Unfortunately, many Americans have very inadequate company pensions once they reach retirement age. In fact, some lack any pension at all. Social Security serves to protect, in a limited way, those who have not planned, or have not had the financial flexibility to save, for the years when they would be physically unable to work. The anticipation of receiving Social Security benefits has probably caused scores of individuals to prepare inadequately for their golden years.

The knowledge of a few acronyms is critical to understanding how the programs commonly referred to as Social Security work in the

THE HISTORY OF THE FICA PAYROLL TAX

CALENDAR YEARS	MAXIMUM EARNINGS SUBJECT TO TAX	MATCHING EMPLOYER AND EMPLOYEE CONTRIBUTIONS AS A PERCENT OF THE CONTRIBUTION BASE			
		OASI	DI	HI	TOTAL
1937-49	$ 3,000	1.000%			1.000%
1950	3,000	1.500			1.500
1951-53	3,600	1.500			1.500
1954	3,600	2.000			2.000
1955-56	4,200	2.000			2.000
1957-58	4,200	2.000	0.250%		2.250
1959	4,800	2.250	0.250		2.500
1960-61	4,800	2.750	0.250		3.000
1962	4,800	2.875	0.250		3.125
1963-65	4,800	3.375	0.250		3.625
1966	6,600	3.500	0.350	0.350%	4.200
1967	6,600	3.550	0.350	0.500	4.400
1968	7,800	3.325	0.475	0.600	4.400
1969	7,800	3.725	0.475	0.600	4.800
1970	7,800	3.650	0.550	0.600	4.800
1971	7,800	4.050	0.550	0.600	5.200
1972	9,000	4.050	0.550	0.600	5.200
1973	10,800	4.300	0.550	1.000	5.850
1974	13,200	4.375	0.575	0.900	5.850
1975	14,100	4.375	0.575	0.900	5.850
1976	15,300	4.375	0.575	0.900	5.850
1977	16,500	4.375	0.575	0.900	5.850
1978	17,700	4.275	0.775	1.000	6.050
1979	22,900	4.330	0.750	1.050	6.130
1980	25,900	4.520	0.560	1.050	6.130
1981	29,700	4.700	0.650	1.300	6.650
1982	32,400	4.575	0.825	1.300	6.700
1983	35,700	4.775	0.625	1.300	6.700
1984	37,800	5.200	0.500	1.300	7.000
1985	39,600	5.200	0.500	1.350	7.050
1986	42,000	5.200	0.500	1.450	7.150
1987	43,800	5.200	0.500	1.450	7.150
1988	45,000	5.530	0.530	1.450	7.510
1989	48,000	5.530	0.530	1.450	7.510
1990	51,300	5.600	0.600	1.450	7.650
1991	53,400*	5.600	0.600	1.450	7.650

* Beginning in 1991, the maximum earnings subject to the Hospital Insurance (Medicare) portion of the FICA tax is substantially higher. This ceiling is $125,000 in 1991.

U.S. today. The majority of Social Security revenues come from the FICA payroll tax, which is levied at a flat rate. This rate has been periodically adjusted to meet the funding needs of a given time period. The FICA tax finances three Social Security trust funds: the Old Age and Survivors Insurance (OASI) Trust Fund, the Disability Insurance (DI) Trust Fund, and the Hospital Insurance (HI) Trust Fund. The largest portion of the tax goes into the OASI Trust Fund.

The OASI program is the largest of the Social Security system, and the one with which most people are familiar. It is, in actuality, a retirement income program, and dates to the original Social Security Act of 1935. OASI cash benefits are paid only to retirees and their eligible dependents and survivors. Eligibility for benefits is based on the amount that a worker contributed into the Social Security program. Those

OASI AND DI PROGRAMS
BENEFICIARIES AND MONTHLY BENEFITS

December 1989

	NUMBER OF PARTICIPANTS (thousands)	AVERAGE MONTHLY BENEFIT
Retired Workers	24,327	$ 567
Wives/husbands of retired workers	3,093	293
Children of retired workers	423	242
Disabled workers	2,895	556
Wives/husbands of disabled workers	271	144
Children of disabled workers	962	157
Widowed mothers and fathers	312	388
Surviving children	1,780	385
Widows and Widowers	4,969	522
Disabled widows/widowers	102	367
Other	16	NA
TOTAL	39,151	$ 512

Source: Social Security Administration

individuals who did not contribute, including some government workers with different publicly-funded retirement plans, are ineligible for OASI benefits.

The DI program provides income security to eligible individuals, under age 65, who are physically or mentally unable to earn a living by working. All people eligible to receive OASI benefits are eligible for DI program benefits. Certain dependents of disabled workers are also entitled to benefits under the DI program. The program pays monthly cash benefits.

The HI program is popularly known as Medicare. It is the third of three insurance trust funds financed by the FICA tax and, beginning in 1991, will be levied on a maximum earnings base of $125,000, substantially higher than the maximum base for the OASI and DI programs. Unlike the OASI and DI programs, Medicare does not provide regular cash benefit payments. Instead, it functions like most other medical insurance programs, paying benefits as claims are incurred. Medicare is split into two separate benefit programs: Part A and Part B. All Americans eligible for monthly Social Security or railroad retirement cash benefits are automatically entitled to benefits under Part A of the Medicare program. Individuals who are not automatically eligible for Part A benefits may join the program by paying an annual premium. Part A is the Hospital Insurance component, into which FICA contributions are paid. Benefits include inpatient hospital care, skilled nursing facility care, home health care, and hospice care, each with certain limitations. Part B of Medicare provides more comprehensive health protection for the elderly, but requires the payment by participants of a monthly premium, which was $29.90 at the beginning of 1991. Part B coverage includes 80 percent of the reasonable charges, after a $100 annual deductible, for covered services. The covered services include most doctors' services, laboratory and diagnostic tests, X-rays, and other health services.

Unlike OASI and DI, the HI program costs far exceed the amount of annual tax contributions into the HI Trust Fund. Costs under this program have risen sharply in recent years, and represent one of the fastest growing items in the Federal budget.

The mechanics of FICA receipts are quite simple. The payroll tax is levied on employees, with a matching amount required to come from the employer. No additional taxes must be paid once the maximum taxable earnings base has been reached. In 1991, the maximum earnings base was established at $53,400 ($125,000 for the Hospital Insurance portion of the tax). The tax rate, paid by both the employee out of gross earnings, and by the employer from separate funds, is 7.65% of the gross earnings of the employee. Self-employed individuals must pay both the employer and employee shares of the tax, for a total rate of 15.3%, on gross earnings below the maximum earnings ceiling.

With the expansion of the retired population, and the constant advance of inflation, the annual cost of the OASI program has skyrocketed. But what we have seen to date is only the tip of the iceberg. In 1990, it was estimated that there were almost 32 million U.S. citizens over the age of 65, or 12% of the total population. In 2010, it is projected that almost 40 million Americans will be over the age of 65, representing 14% of the population, or 1 retired person for every 4.6 people of working age (18-64).

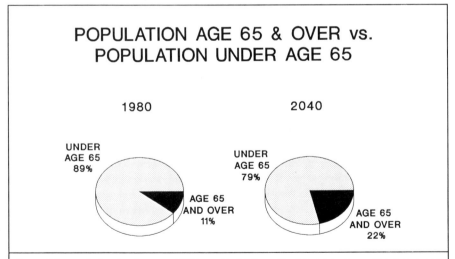

POPULATION AGE 65 & OVER vs. POPULATION UNDER AGE 65

1980

UNDER AGE 65
89%

AGE 65 AND OVER
11%

2040

UNDER AGE 65
79%

AGE 65 AND OVER
22%

Note: The statistics for the year 2040 are Social Security Administration estimates, based on intermediate projections.

Source: 1990 Annual Report of the Federal Old Age and Survivors Insurance and Disability Insurance Trust Funds

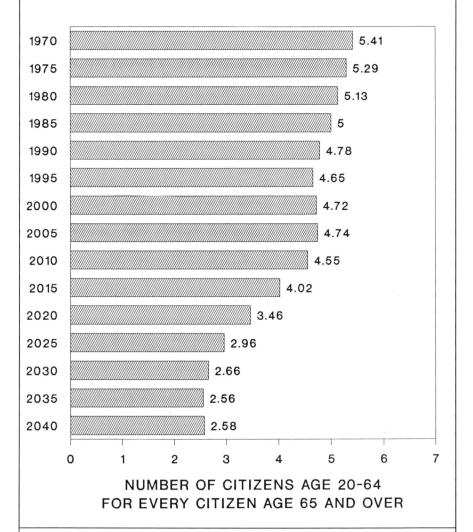

HOW MANY WORKING AGE PEOPLE WILL BE AVAILABLE TO SUPPORT EACH RETIRED PERSON?

Year	Value
1970	5.41
1975	5.29
1980	5.13
1985	5
1990	4.78
1995	4.65
2000	4.72
2005	4.74
2010	4.55
2015	4.02
2020	3.46
2025	2.96
2030	2.66
2035	2.56
2040	2.58

NUMBER OF CITIZENS AGE 20-64
FOR EVERY CITIZEN AGE 65 AND OVER

Note: Data for 1990-2040 are based on estimates reflecting SSA intermediate projections.

Source: Social Security Administration

The cost of maintaining the OASI program is projected to continue its unprecedented rise. For this reason, the Federal Government dramatically increased the FICA tax rate in 1983. The earnings base on which the tax is paid is indexed for inflation, and the OASI Trust Fund is projected to build a large surplus until 2035, when the accumulated surplus will begin to decline gradually.

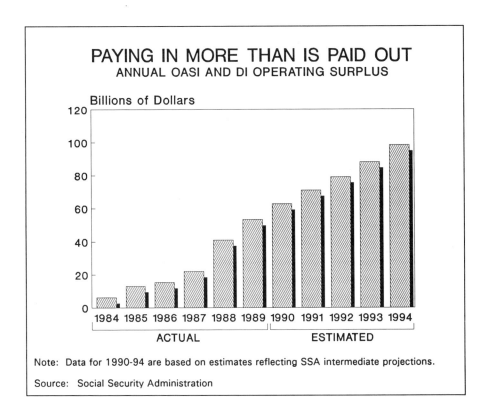

PAYING IN MORE THAN IS PAID OUT
ANNUAL OASI AND DI OPERATING SURPLUS

Billions of Dollars

1984 1985 1986 1987 1988 1989 1990 1991 1992 1993 1994

ACTUAL   ESTIMATED

Note: Data for 1990-94 are based on estimates reflecting SSA intermediate projections.

Source: Social Security Administration

Social Security and the Budget Deficit

Planning for the future is commendable and financially virtuous, and Congress should be saluted for looking ahead and establishing such a large cash reserve to take care of our elderly citizens in the next century. But the surpluses currently being produced distort the actual picture. The large budget deficit that the Government has been running for the past few years has been financed, in part, by the surplus that has been accruing in the Social Security trust funds.

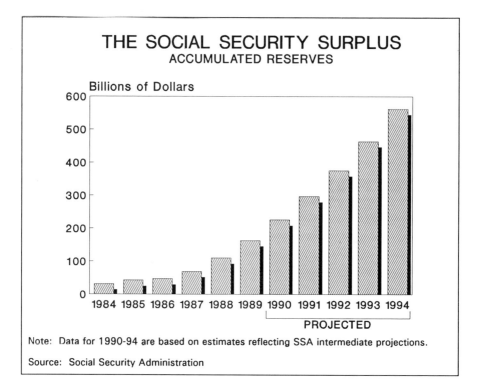

THE SOCIAL SECURITY SURPLUS
ACCUMULATED RESERVES

Billions of Dollars

Note: Data for 1990-94 are based on estimates reflecting SSA intermediate projections.

Source: Social Security Administration

FICA receipts are supposed to be segregated, at least in theory, from the rest of the Federal revenue stream. This sequestration is often dropped, for calculation purposes, when the Federal deficit size is announced by Government officials. The current practice is to refer to certain of the Social Security trust funds as being "off-budget", but to include them when figuring the total budget deficit. Unlike the general operations of the Government, several of the Social Security trust funds are currently in the position to amass major surpluses each year. These surpluses are subsequently used in the debt calculation to reduce the deficit figure which is usually quoted by politicians and the press.

Generating a surplus in the Social Security fund is admirable, as mentioned earlier, if it is used to fund future benefit payments. In fact, the OASI Trust Fund does not hold large cash balances or a diversified investment portfolio. Its only holdings are U.S. Government securities. Each year, when the regular part of the Federal budget shows a deficit, the first Treasury securities sold are purchased by the Social Security trust funds out of the annual surplus. Consequently, when Social Security tax revenues are not sufficient to meet benefit payments sometime next century, the Federal Government will have to look elsewhere to find the cash to make up the difference. New taxes or bonds will be necessary to fund future benefit payments. That means today's FICA tax really is a tax to fund today's expenses; not only Social Security, but any other deficit expenditures in the general Federal budget that a Social Security surplus can cover.

The problem with using the FICA tax surplus as a supplement to income tax revenues is that it is a regressive tax. A generally accepted taxation concept in this country is that those most able to pay tax should pay the most for the funding of government activities. Our income tax is progressive: an individual making $70,000 pays a higher percentage of his or her income in the form of Federal income taxes than does an individual making $20,000. Simply applying the FICA tax to all income would make it a flat tax, with taxpayers paying the same portion of their income to the FICA trust funds. But because FICA tax is subject to a maximum earnings ceiling, those earning the highest incomes actually pay a smaller percentage of their income in the form of an FICA tax than do taxpayers earning the lowest incomes.

1990 AVERAGE FICA TAX RATES UNDER 3 INCOME SCENARIOS

1990 Ceiling on income subject
to the FICA tax was $51,300

ANNUAL TAXABLE INCOME	FICA TAXES PAID	AVERAGE FICA TAX RATE
$ 25,000	$1,912.50	7.65 %
$ 75,000	$3,924.45	5.23 %
$150,000	$3,924.45	2.62 %

The Affordability of the Social Security Program

According to the rules of eligibility, only those workers that have paid into the Social Security program, through FICA taxes, are eligible to receive benefits. But despite the fact that workers, in essence, pay premiums into this "insurance" program, there should be no illusions about its similarity to a systematic investment scheme. Social Security is unquestionably the largest welfare program in the world, and really bears little resemblance to conventional insurance. It provides benefits that are far in excess of the contributions that even the highest wage earners pay into the program. The actual "return on investment" for those who contribute is so high that it would undoubtedly surpass any other investment return that might otherwise have been available to the individual. If it were allowable, we would be foolish not to invest all of our spare cash in the Social Security program.

An examination of some figures will illustrate the point. Let's assume that Ed Fisher retired in 1990 after working for 41 years. Ed was a fortunate man - he earned a relatively high salary throughout his life, which always exceeded the maximum base subject to the FICA tax. As required, his employer also contributed the maximum to Social Security on Ed's behalf. Through the years, each contributed $27,802.50, for a total of $55,605.00. For this pool of contributed capital, Ed was eligible to begin receiving benefits, which were $11,753 in 1990. These benefits would continue until both Ed and his wife died, and would always be adjusted to account for increases in the cost of living.

If Ed and his wife lived until Ed reached age 80, which would represent a full 15 years of retirement and Social Security benefits, he could conceivably take out more than four times his total actual contributions to Social Security. Even if his contribution pool had been invested and grown at a rate of 5% over the entire period, beginning with his first FICA tax payment, Ed's probable benefits would still be 2.75 times the accumulated balance at the start of his retirement.

This "investment" in Social Security compares very favorably with what Ed might have been able to receive in retirement if he had opted not to contribute to Social Security (which isn't legal), and had alternatively invested similar amounts on his own. If Ed's contributions into this private investment program had paralleled the contributions that both he and his employer had paid into Social Security, and these funds had grown at an annual rate of 5%, his retirement nest egg would be second-rate compared to his Social Security insurance. If we assume mortality at age 80, cost of living increases each year, and the gradual use of the accumulated investment principal to pay annual benefits, Ed's personal security program would pay a benefit of $7,878 in 1990. Such a benefit would be 33% less than the 1990 Social Security benefit, and the shortfall would only grow larger over time.

ED FISHER IN RETIREMENT

Contributions to Social Security, 1949-1989:

Ed, through payroll taxes	$27,802.50
Ed's employer, at matching rate	$27,802.50
Total Contributions	$55,605.00

Value of Social Security contributions at end of 1989, if balances were invested, and grew at 5% per year: $92,000.00

Annual Social Security Benefit beginning in 1990: $11,753.00

Balanced annual draw on investment beginning in 1990, if invested same amounts outside of Social Security, allowing for 5% annual increases: $7,878.00

The Future of Social Security

Many Americans are skeptical about the likelihood of Social Security's long term survival. However, cancellation of the program,

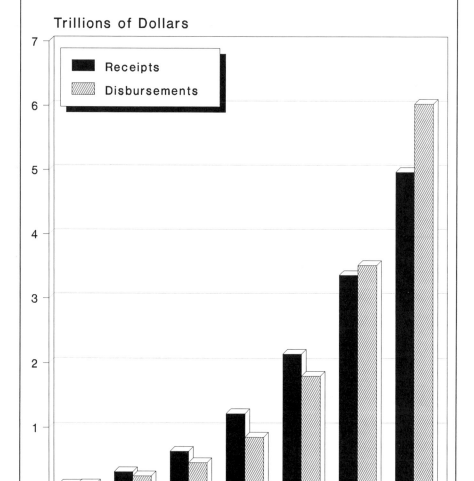

THE SOLVENCY OF SOCIAL SECURITY
MONEY IN VS. MONEY OUT

Trillions of Dollars

Receipts

Disbursements

1980 1990 2000 2010 2020 2030 2040

Note: Data for 1990-2040 are based on estimates reflecting SSA intermediate projections.

Source: Social Security Administration

which provides much needed benefits to the elderly poor, is not on the political or social horizon.

But Social Security is so generous to its beneficiaries that it is unlikely the program, as it is currently defined, will be affordable over the longer term. The size of the current Social Security entitlement, and the expected future cost of the program, make it ripe for reform. Many wealthy individuals, who receive the benefit simply because they meet the age requirement, hardly need the income to support their retirement. Yet, the facts that the OASI and DI programs are self-funding, and currently generating large surpluses, will be cited as evidence to support the argument that the current level of benefits is sustainable, and indeed affordable, for the taxpayer.

All elements of taxation must be viewed in the larger context, and as a whole. If the electorate is willing to be taxed at a certain overall level, then an allocation of an unnecessarily large portion of that tax rate to an overly generous welfare/retirement program takes away the opportunity for the Federal Government to fund other programs, or perhaps balance the budget, with those tax dollars.

Many options for reform are possible. Phasing out benefits for wealthier and higher income retirees is a first step. Fully taxing Social Security benefit payments is another option. Limiting the level of annual cost of living adjustments would slow program growth. Eliminating early retirement options would encourage people to work longer, allowing a greater earnings period to enhance retirement savings, and ultimately reduce dependency upon Social Security benefits.

Medicare is a different story. The cost of this program has surprised even the best policymakers, but reforms are possible here, too. Medicare coverage could also be phased out for wealthier people. Premiums for Part B could be increased, to more accurately reflect the actuarial cost of covering the elderly, typically very intense users of the national health care system.

As is true with much of the Federal operation, a fresh approach is needed to our safety net for the retired and elderly community. When the existing paradigms are tossed aside, it will be possible to bring the programs back to where they originally were intended to be. The overall affordability of these programs must be critically examined. Most probably, an across-the-board reduction in benefits will be an appropriate course of action.

OPINION BUILDERS

1. *Does the extraordinary annual expense of the Social Security system warrant significant overhaul of the program, or is it simply a burden which society should willingly accept?*

2. *Are Social Security benefits too high, too low, or just right?*

3. *Should Social Security benefits be based upon need? If so, what guidelines should be used to determine need?*

4. *Should Social Security benefits be available to those who choose to retire early, or should benefits kick in only at a predetermined age such as 65?*

5. *Has the Social Security program grown so large that it now represents a program that is technically impossible to continue funding?*

6. *Do elderly and retired Americans exert too much influence on Members of Congress when it comes to Social Security benefits? Has adequate public debate on the funding of Social Security been forced under the rug in recent years?*

7. *Considering the maximum contributions that might have been made into the Social Security program during working years by those currently in retirement, are the benefits being paid too high?*

8. *Is it possible that Social Security could become as big a thorn in the side of the Federal Government as deposit insurance has, given the huge liability of the program and the current limited reserves?*

CHAPTER TEN

THE HIGH COST OF NATIONAL DEFENSE

The Price of Protecting the World

The need to maintain a strong defense capability has rarely been questioned in this nation since the Japanese attacked Pearl Harbor. That historic event wrenched the U.S. from its isolationism, and put the country on a course which resulted in the emergence of the U.S. as a superpower. Along the way, isolationism was quickly forgotten, as America attempted to extend its influence worldwide.

Much of the scramble for world influence can be traced to the perceived need to contain the communist threat to people around the world, which seemed to spread in the post-World War II era. The democratic history of our government, founded on the basis of popular participation and opinion, is in direct contrast to the form which communism assumed in the twentieth century in places like the Soviet Union and China. These countries suppressed personal will, belief, and ambition, unless it followed the doctrine preached by the ruling elite. In most cases, communist countries were ruled by dictators, rather than the type of communist leader that might have emerged from the purest interpretations of communist doctrine.

The "communist threat" was very real. In post-war Europe, a number of eastern European countries were brought forcefully under

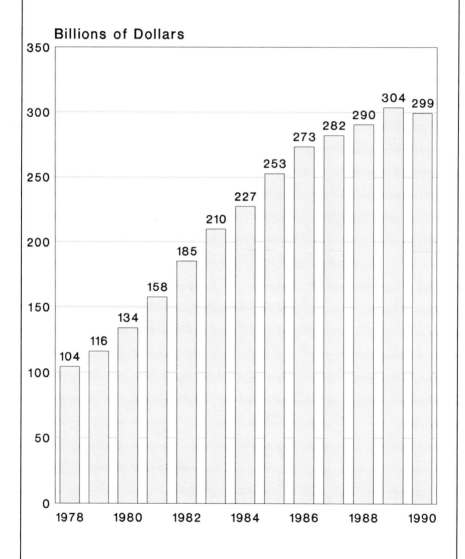

DEFENSE EXPENDITURES
1978-1990

Billions of Dollars

Source: Office of Management and Budget

communist control with the aid of the Soviet Union, and the appetite for more influence seemed high on the Soviet agenda. Communist regimes were supported by the Soviets in all parts of the world. The Chinese were similarly active in Asia. The U.S. fought in the Korean War and the Vietnam War to contain the spread of communism.

The formation of the United Nations in 1945 established a permanent world body to pursue international peace. The United States, after aiding European countries in defeating Nazi Germany, and defeating the imperialistic Japanese, rose to a high level of international influence. With that influence came a formalized responsibility to aid in the protection of democratically inclined nations, and to contain communism.

The North Atlantic Treaty Organization (NATO) was founded in 1949. Its membership includes most Western European countries, plus the United States, Canada, and Iceland. Signatories to the treaty agreed to regard an attack on any one member country as an attack on all member countries, which sent a signal to the expansionist Soviet empire that no further territorial encroachment would be tolerated.

In the battle of influence which followed World War II, arms development and proliferation became the centerpiece. The Cold War became a national obsession in the 1950s, and continues today. The Cold War has been characterized as a period of relative peace, compared to the two earlier World Wars, but has clearly been a war of nerves and technology. Weapons innovation and stockpiled military arsenals became the most important way to assert influence.

The cost of the defense superiority strategy has been very great. Pentagon officials worked feverishly to initiate new weapons development programs that might leapfrog the U.S. ahead of Soviet military technology. At the end of the 1970s, and through the 1980s, the U.S. embarked upon an unprecedented buildup of military strength. President Reagan waged a war of rhetoric against the Soviet Union in the early 1980s, calling it an "Evil Empire" and rallying support for the continuing peacetime arms buildup.

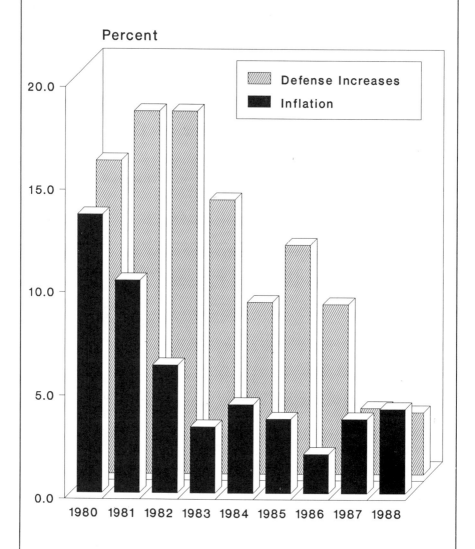

DEFENSE SPENDING INCREASES COMPARED TO THE INFLATION RATE

Note: Inflation is measured as change in the Consumer Price Index.

Sources: Office of Management and Budget and Bureau of Labor Statistics

Defense spending nearly tripled between 1977 and 1987, with slower growth after 1987. The defense budgets of the 1980s are now history, but these spending blueprints contributed in a significant way to the increase in Federal debt obligations.

The virtual collapse of Soviet-enforced communism in Eastern Europe at the end of 1989 led many politicians and government analysts to publicly predict the dismantling of the American military. Huge cuts in the military budgets were anticipated, and free-spending members of Congress coveted the "Peace Dividend." The Cold War was over, the Soviets had lost, communism had been defeated by the will of the people, the need for ongoing battle readiness was significantly diminished, and military spending would be substantially reduced. Or so the argument went.

Once again, our politicians were counting their chickens after they had already been given away. With a budget deficit for FY 1989 that weighed in at $153 billion ($206 billion if the Social Security surplus is excluded), it is difficult to understand from where this supposed "Peace Dividend" would be coming. Simple math exercises could easily prove that cutting the FY 1989 defense spending of $303 billion in half would barely eliminate the already existing budget deficit. In fact, there would be no Peace Dividend unless the entire military machine was dismantled.

Defense spending did decline 1% from 1989 to 1990. Far from being a dividend, this piece of fiscal thrift was lost in the overall Federal deficit for FY 1990, which measured $220 billion.

As 1990 dragged on, it became very clear that a substantial reduction in defense spending was unlikely at any time in the foreseeable future. Two different situations in the world served as supporting evidence that aided Pentagon officials who were trying to prevent a military demobilization.

The first mitigating development was the declining power of the moderate Soviet reformist, President Mikhail Gorbachev. Inadequate results from economic freedoms which had been granted in the Soviet economy weakened his position within his own political hierarchy, and

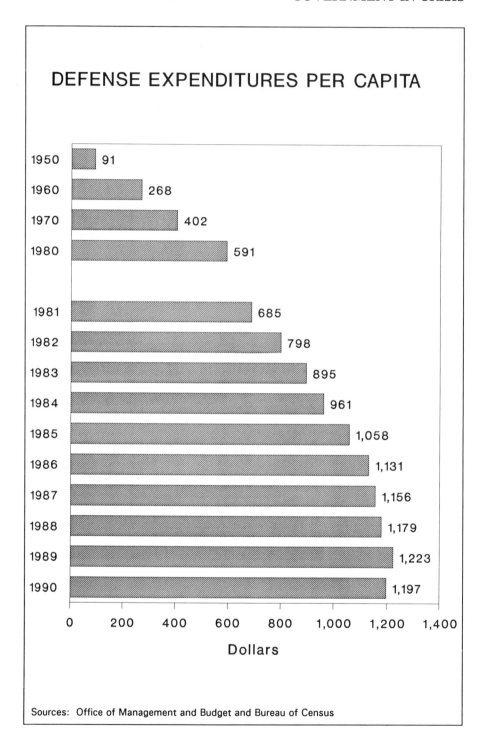

DEFENSE EXPENDITURES PER CAPITA

Year	Dollars
1950	91
1960	268
1970	402
1980	591
1981	685
1982	798
1983	895
1984	961
1985	1,058
1986	1,131
1987	1,156
1988	1,179
1989	1,223
1990	1,197

Dollars

Sources: Office of Management and Budget and Bureau of Census

he began to be viewed in some quarters as being too eager to lead the Soviet Union into a western-style government. Conservative communist party forces and key military personnel were reported to be against further rapid reform. Additionally, these quarters continued to push for strong action against independence-minded Soviet republics, such as the Baltic states of Lithuania, Latvia, and Estonia, and other republics such as Armenia. The possible reemergence of conservative ideologues in a post-Gorbachev Soviet Union, and a parallel resumption of Cold War practices by a new regime, has already caused numerous officials in the U.S. to mount strong protests against cuts in defense appropriations.

The second and more obvious need for a strong American military capability came with Iraq's invasion of neighboring Kuwait. The need to maintain the balance of world oil power, coupled with a desire to prevent the uninvited domination of one country by another, led to a rapid buildup of U.S. military forces in the Persian Gulf region. It was obvious that a redeployment so rapid and so massive was only possible with a large, costly, and ongoing military machine. After resolutions and ultimatums were passed by the United Nations, Saddam Hussein's continued defiance prompted the start of the Persian Gulf War.

The war in the Persian Gulf region had important military and economic lessons for the American government. Clearly, no other country was capable of constructing a military operation as formidable in such a short period of time. The war also proved the effectiveness of American military equipment and strategy. Additionally, the war illustrated the immense cost of waging a modern high technology war, requiring not only sophisticated and costly weaponry, but also a large personnel deployment. With the U.S. goals for the war parallel to the desires of many other nations, the offers of financial assistance for the military came fast. Third party governments demonstrated a willingness to pay a share of the expenses incurred by the U.S. military in such an operation. The commitments by several economically powerful countries, notably the wealthy Kuwaiti government-in-exile, Saudi Arabia, Germany, and Japan, meant that much of the cost of the war would be borne by foreign governments.

In the end, the cost of the American part of the coalition military effort to liberate Kuwait is expected to be between $40 billion and $60 billion. The financial and material support received from other countries offset the cost of the war actually borne by the American taxpayer. This support totaled approximately $55 billion - enough to pay for most of the operation. But despite the resulting low cost to the U.S. for leading the Allies in the waging of the war, the cost to be ready to participate in such a war remained the same to U.S. taxpayers.

THE PERSIAN GULF WAR

FINANCIAL AND MATERIAL COMMITMENTS FROM COALITION COUNTRIES FOR THE SUPPORT OF THE U.S. MILITARY EFFORT

TOTAL EXPECTED COST
OF THE AMERICAN PART
OF THE MILITARY EFFORT $40-60 billion

FINANCIAL AND MATERIAL COMMITMENTS:

Saudi Arabia	$ 16.8 B
Kuwait	16.0
Japan	10.7
Germany	6.5
United Arab Emirates	4.0
South Korea	0.4
TOTAL	$54.5 B

Notes: Some donors have put restrictions on the types of expenses that can be funded with committed money. Numbers do not add due to rounding.

Source: Senate Armed Services Committee.

If, in the New World Order, the United States is to be the keeper of democratic freedoms and champion of universal economic opportunity, then a strong military will be necessary. When the American military is called upon to thwart a power-hungry dictator, bent on domination, the world may be very willing to support the cause financially and, in some instances, militarily. But it is unclear whether these same nations, so grateful that we can come to the rescue of distressed regions, are willing to foot the bill for the peace-time maintenance of U.S. military might. If they are not, and if the United States is inclined to assume the leadership role in the New World Order, then it is doubtful that U.S. military expenditures will decline sizably at any time in the future.

OPINION BUILDERS

1. *Is the amount of money that is being spent on defense activities, in absolute dollars, too high, too low, or just right?*

2. *Do you believe that the U.S should take an active or passive role in world affairs?*

3. *If you believe that the U.S. should have an active role in world affairs, do you believe that the periodic use of military power is an appropriate way to preserve a position of leadership?*

4. *Do you believe that the participation of the U.S. military in the following areas was appropriate or inappropriate?*

Grenada	*1987*
Panama	*1989*
Kuwait	*1990-91*

5. *Considering the events that led up to the Persian Gulf War and the war itself, do you believe that there is sufficient reason to expect a large-scale demobilization of the U.S. military?*

CHAPTER ELEVEN

BALANCE THE BUDGET YOURSELF

Could You Be An Effective Member of Congress?

Most of us have criticized Congress at one time or another for its inability to straighten out the budget fiasco. As discussed, the Federal budget is large and complicated, mirroring the far-reaching operations of the Federal Government. It is probably not a question of raising taxes or limiting spending, but instead a question of integrating the two approaches.

The ultimate strategic policy dilemma is this: How much do we want from the government, and how much are we willing to pay? It is just another way of asking the question: How much can we afford?

Let's take the finances of the Federal Government into our own hands, literally. Assume that it is best to have a balanced budget for the purpose of this exercise. We will examine specific revenues and expenditures from fiscal year 1990, and operate as "Monday-morning-quarterbacks," enjoying the benefit of hindsight.

For this exercise, we will consider the Social Security trust funds untouchable. The surpluses being run in these programs are for building reserves to pay future benefits, and really should be allowed to accrue peacefully and undisturbed. They are not an option when deciding how to pay down the deficit.

Our mission is to raise revenues where appropriate, and eliminate or reduce categories of expenditure, until we have balanced the budget. The goal is to find $277 billion.

Due to the immense amount of detail in the budget, we will need to take more of a summary perspective. Some richness will be lost in the process, but many sub-programs are relatively easy to identify, even when grouped with supervisory programs and not specifically referenced.

Three columns will be provided for your budget-balancing exercise. It is likely that your first-pass cuts will add up to much less than you expected. If that is the case, try again - be as tough as you need to be to cover the remaining shortfall. If you fail a second time, repeat the exercise once more, this time waving your budget axe more cavalierly. Good luck! If you succeed, you might seriously consider a candidacy in the next Congressional race in your district.

THE BUDGET-BALANCING EXERCISE

THE FINANCES OF THE FEDERAL GOVERNMENT
FISCAL YEAR 1990

TOTAL REVENUES: $749.6 Billion
TOTAL EXPENDITURES: $1,026.6 Billion

TOTAL DEFICIT: $277.0 Billion

Directions:

Examine the following budget categories and actual 1990 amounts, and propose new spending and tax receipt levels such that the 1990 deficit of $277 Billion is eliminated.

Use the first column to write the amount of any proposed budget category cut or revenue increase, keeping careful, page-by-page totals. At the end, record the page totals on the summary sheet, again using the first column. If your budget adjustments do not eliminate the deficit, try again, this time using the second column. A third column is provided for those that need it.

EXPENDITURE CATEGORIES	ACTUAL EXPENDITURES ($ Billions)	SPENDING CUTS		
		1	2	3
1. NATIONAL DEFENSE:				
Department of Defense - Military:				
Military personnel	75.6			
Operation and Maintenance	88.3	____	____	____
Procurement	81.0	____	____	____
Research, development, test and evaluation	37.5	____	____	____
Military construction	5.1	____	____	____
Family housing	3.5	____	____	____
Allowances & Receipts	-1.2	____	____	____
Subtotal	289.8			
Atomic energy defense activities	9.0	____	____	____
Defense-related activities	0.6	____	____	____
TOTAL	**299.3**	____	____	____

EXPENDITURE CATEGORIES	ACTUAL EXPENDITURES ($ Billions)	SPENDING CUTS		
		1	2	3
2. GENERAL SCIENCE, SPACE, AND TECHNOLOGY:				
General Science and basic research:				
National Science Foundation programs	1.8	____	____	____
Department of Energy general science programs	<u>1.0</u>	____	____	____
Subtotal	2.8	____	____	____
Space Flight	7.4	____	____	____
Space science, applications, and technology	3.1	____	____	____
Supporting space activities	1.1	____	____	____
TOTAL	**14.4**	____	____	____

EXPENDITURE CATEGORIES	ACTUAL EXPENDITURES ($ Billions)	SPENDING CUTS		
		1	2	3
3. INTERNATIONAL AFFAIRS:				
International development and humanitarian assistance:				
Agency for International Development	2.6	___	___	___
Multilateral Development Banks	1.4	___	___	___
Food aid	1.0	___	___	___
Refugee Programs	0.5	___	___	___
Voluntary contributions to international organizations	0.3	___	___	___
State Department narcotics assistance	0.1	___	___	___
Peace Corps	0.2	___	___	___
Receipts	-0.6	___	___	___
Subtotal	5.5	___	___	___
International Security Assistance:				
Foreign military financing	4.7	___	___	___
Economic Support Fund	3.7	___	___	___
Other programs	0.5	___	___	___
Offsetting receipts	-0.2	___	___	___
Subtotal	8.7	___	___	___
Conduct of Foreign Affairs:				
State Department salaries and expenses	1.8	___	___	___
Foreign buildings	0.4	___	___	___
United Nations programs	0.7	___	___	___
Other programs	0.1	___	___	___
Subtotal	3.1	___	___	___

EXPENDITURE CATEGORIES	ACTUAL EXPENDITURES ($ Billions)	SPENDING CUTS		
		1	2	3
Foreign information and exchange activities:				
U.S. Information Agency	0.9	___	___	___
Board for International Broadcasting	0.2	___	___	___
Subtotal	1.1	___	___	___
International financial programs:				
Export-Import Bank	0.4	___	___	___
Net other programs and offsetting receipts	-4.9	___	___	___
Subtotal	-4.5	___	___	___
TOTAL	**13.8**	___	___	___

EXPENDITURE CATEGORIES	ACTUAL EXPENDITURES ($ Billions)	SPENDING CUTS		
		1	2	3
4. ENERGY:				
Energy Supply:				
Research and development	2.5	___	___	___
Petroleum reserves	-0.4	___	___	___
Federal power marketing	-0.7	___	___	___
Tennessee Valley Authority	-0.4	___	___	___
Uranium enrichment	-0.1	___	___	___
Nuclear waste program	0.3	___	___	___
Nuclear waste fund receipts	-0.6	___	___	___
Subsidies for non-conventional fuel production	0.1	___	___	___
Rural electric and telephone	0.3	___	___	___
Subtotal	1.0	___	___	___
Energy conservation grants & R&D	0.4	___	___	___
Emergency Energy Preparedness	0.4	___	___	___
Energy information, policy, and regulation:				
Nuclear Regulatory Commission	0.2	___	___	___
Other energy programs	0.3	___	___	___
Subtotal	0.6	___	___	___
TOTAL	**2.4**	___	___	___

EXPENDITURE CATEGORIES	ACTUAL EXPENDITURES ($ Billions)	SPENDING CUTS		
		1	2	3

5. AGRICULTURE:

Farm income stabilization:

Commodity Credit Corporation	6.4	_____	_____	_____
Crop insurance	1.0	_____	_____	_____
Agricultural credit insurance	2.2	_____	_____	_____
Temporary emergency food assistance program	<u>0.2</u>	_____	_____	_____
Subtotal	9.8	_____	_____	_____

Agricultural research and services:

Research programs	1.0	_____	_____	_____
Extension programs	0.4	_____	_____	_____
Marketing programs	0.2	_____	_____	_____
Animal and plant health programs	0.4	_____	_____	_____
Economic intelligence	0.2	_____	_____	_____
Net other programs and offsetting receipts	<u>0.1</u>	_____	_____	_____
Subtotal	2.2	_____	_____	_____
TOTAL	**12.0**	_____	_____	_____

EXPENDITURE CATEGORIES	ACTUAL EXPENDITURES ($ Billions)	SPENDING CUTS		
		1	2	3

6. NATURAL RESOURCES AND ENVIRONMENT:

Water Resources:

Corps of Engineers	3.5	___	___	___
Bureau of Reclamation	1.0	___	___	___
Net other programs and offsetting receipts	-0.1	___	___	___
Subtotal	4.4	___	___	___

Conservation and land management:

Management of national forests, cooperative forestry, and forestry research	2.5	___	___	___
Management of public lands	0.8	___	___	___
Mining reclamation and enforcement	0.3	___	___	___
Conservation reserve program	1.5	___	___	___
Other conservation of agricultural lands	0.7	___	___	___
Net other programs and offsetting receipts	-2.3	___	___	___
Subtotal	3.6	___	___	___

Recreational Resources:

Federal land acquisition	0.2	___	___	___
Operation of recreational resources	1.7	___	___	___
Net other programs and offsetting receipts	-0.1	___	___	___
Subtotal	1.9	___	___	___

EXPENDITURE CATEGORIES	ACTUAL EXPENDITURES ($ Billions)	SPENDING CUTS		
		1	2	3
Pollution control and abatement:				
Regulatory, enforcement, and research programs	1.7	_____	_____	_____
Hazardous substance response fund	1.1	_____	_____	_____
Sewage treatment plants construction grants	2.3	_____	_____	_____
Leaking underground storage tank trust fund	0.1	_____	_____	_____
Net other programs and offsetting receipts	-0.1	_____	_____	_____
Subtotal	5.2	_____	_____	_____
Other programs	2.1	_____	_____	_____
TOTAL	17.1	_____	_____	_____

EXPENDITURE CATEGORIES	ACTUAL EXPENDITURES ($ Billions)	SPENDING CUTS		
		1	2	3

7. COMMERCE AND HOUSING CREDIT:

Mortgage Credit:				
Mortgage backed securities	-0.5	___	___	___
Mortgage credit	1.0	___	___	___
Housing for elderly or handicapped	0.3	___	___	___
Rural housing programs	3.0	___	___	___
Subtotal	3.8	___	___	___
Payments to Postal Service Fund	0.5	___	___	___
Deposit Insurance:				
Resolution Trust Corporation	46.5	___	___	___
Bank Insurance Fund	6.4	___	___	___
FSLIC Insurance Fund	5.2	___	___	___
Savings Association Insurance Fund	0.1	___	___	___
Net other programs	-0.2	___	___	___
Subtotal	58.1	___	___	___
Other advancement of commerce:				
Small and minority business assistance	0.4	___	___	___
Science and technology	0.3	___	___	___
Economic and demographic statistics	1.6	___	___	___
International trade and other	0.8	___	___	___
Subtotal	3.1	___	___	___
TOTAL	**65.5**	___	___	___

EXPENDITURE CATEGORIES	ACTUAL EXPENDITURES ($ Billions)	SPENDING CUTS		
		1	2	3
8. TRANSPORTATION:				
Ground transportation:				
Highways	14.2			
Highway safety	0.4			
Mass transit	3.8			
Railroads	0.5			
Subtotal	19.0			
Air transportation:				
Airports and airways	6.4			
Aeronautical research and technology	0.8			
Subtotal	7.2			
Water transportation:				
Marine safety and transportation	3.0			
Ocean shipping	0.2			
Subtotal	3.2			
Net other programs and offsetting receipts	0.2			
TOTAL	**29.5**			

EXPENDITURE CATEGORIES	ACTUAL EXPENDITURES ($ Billions)	SPENDING CUTS		
		1	2	3

9. EDUCATION, TRAINING, EMPLOYMENT, AND SOCIAL SERVICES:

Elementary, secondary, and vocational education:

School improvement programs	1.2	___	___	___
Compensatory education	4.5	___	___	___
Special education	1.6	___	___	___
Impact aid	0.8	___	___	___
Vocational and adult education	1.3	___	___	___
Other	0.5	___	___	___
Subtotal	9.9	___	___	___

Higher education:

Student financial assistance	5.9	___	___	___
Guaranteed Student Loan program	4.4	___	___	___
Higher education	0.7	___	___	___
Other	0.2	___	___	___
Subtotal	11.1	___	___	___

Research and general education aids	1.6	___	___	___

Training and employment:

Training and employment services	3.8	___	___	___
Older Americans employment	0.3	___	___	___
Federal-State employment service	1.1	___	___	___
Other programs	0.1	___	___	___
Subtotal	5.4	___	___	___

Other labor services	0.8	___	___	___

EXPENDITURE CATEGORIES	ACTUAL EXPENDITURES ($ Billions)	SPENDING CUTS		
		1	2	3
Social Services:				
Social services block grant	2.7	_____	_____	_____
Grants to States for special services	0.4	_____	_____	_____
Rehabilitation services	1.8	_____	_____	_____
Payments to states for foster care and adoption assistance	1.6	_____	_____	_____
Human development services	2.6	_____	_____	_____
Domestic volunteer programs	0.2	_____	_____	_____
Other programs	0.5	_____	_____	_____
Subtotal	9.7	_____	_____	_____
TOTAL	38.5	_____	_____	_____

EXPENDITURE CATEGORIES	ACTUAL EXPENDITURES ($ Billions)	SPENDING CUTS		
		1	2	3
10. COMMUNITY AND REGIONAL DEVELOPMENT:				
Community development:				
Community development block grants	2.8	___	___	___
Other programs	0.7	___	___	___
Subtotal	3.5	___	___	___
Area and regional development:				
Rural development	1.4	___	___	___
Economic development assistance	0.2	___	___	___
Indian programs	1.4	___	___	___
Regional commissions	0.1	___	___	___
Tennessee Valley Authority	0.1	___	___	___
Net other programs and offsetting receipts	-0.3	___	___	___
Subtotal	2.9	___	___	___
Disaster relief and insurance:				
Small business disaster loans	0.3	___	___	___
Disaster relief	1.3	___	___	___
Other programs	0.4	___	___	___
Subtotal	2.1	___	___	___
TOTAL	8.5	___	___	___

EXPENDITURE CATEGORIES	ACTUAL EXPENDITURES ($ Billions)	SPENDING CUTS 1	2	3
11. HEALTH:				
Health care services:				
Medicaid grants	41.1			
Federal employees health benefits	1.6			
Other health care services	4.9			
Subtotal	47.6			
Health Research:				
National Institutes of Health research	7.1			
Other research programs	0.9			
Subtotal	8.0			
Education and training of health care workforce:				
National Institutes of Health research training	0.3			
Clinical training	0.2			
Subtotal	0.6			
Consumer and occupational health safety:				
Consumer safety	1.0			
Occupational safety and health	0.5			
Subtotal	1.5			
TOTAL	**57.7**			

EXPENDITURE CATEGORIES	ACTUAL EXPENDITURES ($ Billions)	SPENDING CUTS		
		1	2	3
12. INCOME SECURITY:				
General retirement and disability insurance:				
Railroad retirement	4.2	___	___	___
Special benefits for disabled coal miners	1.5	___	___	___
Pension Benefit Guaranty Corporation	-0.7	___	___	___
Other	0.1	___	___	___
Subtotal	5.1	___	___	___
Federal employee retirement and disability:				
Civilian retirement and disability programs	31.5	___	___	___
Military retirement	21.5	___	___	___
Federal employees workers' compensation	-0.1	___	___	___
Federal employees life insurance fund	-0.9	___	___	___
Subtotal	52.0	___	___	___
Unemployment compensation	18.9	___	___	___
Housing assistance:				
Subsidized housing	12.8	___	___	___
Public housing operating subsidies	1.8	___	___	___
Low-rent public housing loans	0.4	___	___	___
Transitional housing and emergency shelter for the homeless	0.1	___	___	___
Other housing assistance	0.9	___	___	___
Subtotal	15.9	___	___	___

EXPENDITURE CATEGORIES	ACTUAL EXPENDITURES ($ Billions)	SPENDING CUTS		
		1	2	3
Food and nutrition assistance:				
Food stamps	15.0	_____	_____	_____
Aid to Puerto Rico	0.9	_____	_____	_____
Child nutrition and other programs	8.0	_____	_____	_____
Subtotal	24.0	_____	_____	_____
Other income security:				
Supplemental security income (SSI)	12.6	_____	_____	_____
Family support payments	12.2	_____	_____	_____
JOBS training program for welfare recipients	0.3	_____	_____	_____
Earned income tax credit	4.4	_____	_____	_____
Refugee assistance	0.4	_____	_____	_____
Low income home energy assistance	1.3	_____	_____	_____
Other programs	0.2	_____	_____	_____
Subtotal	31.4	_____	_____	_____
TOTAL	147.3	_____	_____	_____

EXPENDITURE CATEGORIES	ACTUAL EXPENDITURES ($ Billions)	SPENDING CUTS		
		1	2	3

13. VETERANS BENEFITS AND SERVICES:

Income Security for Veterans:

Service-connected compensation	10.7	____	____	____
Non-service connected pensions	3.6	____	____	____
Burial and other benefits	0.1	____	____	____
National service life insurance trust fund	1.2	____	____	____
Net other insurance programs and offsetting receipts	-0.4	____	____	____
Subtotal	15.2	____	____	____

Veterans education, training, and rehabilitation:

Readjustment benefits	0.5	____	____	____
All-volunteer force educational assistance trust fund	-0.2	____	____	____
Subtotal	0.3	____	____	____

Hospital and medical care for veterans:

Medical care and hospital services	11.3	____	____	____
Medical administration, research, and other	0.3	____	____	____
Construction	0.7	____	____	____
Fees and other charges for medical services	-0.1	____	____	____
Subtotal	12.1	____	____	____

EXPENDITURE CATEGORIES	ACTUAL EXPENDITURES ($ Billions)	SPENDING CUTS		
		1	2	3
Veterans housing:				
Loan guaranty revolving fund	0.6	___	___	___
Receipts	<u>-0.1</u>	___	___	___
Subtotal	0.5	___	___	___
Other veterans benefits and services:				
Cemeteries, administration of veterans				
benefits, and other	0.9	___	___	___
Non-VA support programs	<u>0.1</u>	___	___	___
Subtotal	0.9	___	___	___
TOTAL	**29.1**	___	___	___

EXPENDITURE CATEGORIES	ACTUAL EXPENDITURES ($ Billions)	SPENDING CUTS		
		1	2	3
14. SOCIAL SECURITY:				
On-budget only	3.6	_____	_____	_____
15. MEDICARE:				
Hospital insurance (HI)	66.7	_____	_____	_____
Supplementary Medical Insurance (SMI)	43.0	_____	_____	_____
Medicare premiums and collections	-11.6	_____	_____	_____
TOTAL	**98.1**	_____	_____	_____

EXPENDITURE CATEGORIES	ACTUAL EXPENDITURES ($ Billions)	SPENDING CUTS		
		1	2	3

16. ADMINISTRATION OF JUSTICE:

Federal law enforcement activities:				
Criminal investigations (DEA, FBI, FCEN, OCDE)	2.1	___	___	___
Alcohol, tobacco, and firearms investigation (ATF)	0.3	___	___	___
Border enforcement activities	2.2	___	___	___
Customs user fee	-0.9	___	___	___
Protection activities (Secret Service)	0.4	___	___	___
Other enforcement	0.5	___	___	___
Subtotal	4.6	___	___	___
Federal litigative and judicial activities:				
Civil and criminal prosecution and representation	1.6	___	___	___
Federal judicial activities	1.7	___	___	___
Representation of indigents in civil cases	0.3	___	___	___
Subtotal	3.6	___	___	___
Federal correctional activities	1.3	___	___	___
Criminal justice assistance	0.5	___	___	___
TOTAL	**10.0**	___	___	___

EXPENDITURE CATEGORIES	ACTUAL EXPENDITURES ($ Billions)	SPENDING CUTS		
		1	2	3
17. GENERAL GOVERNMENT:				
Legislative functions	1.8			
Executive direction and management	0.2			
Central fiscal operations:				
Collection of taxes	5.4			
Other fiscal operations	<u>0.6</u>			
Subtotal	6.0			
Central personnel management	0.2			
General purpose fiscal assistance:				
Payments and loans to the District of Columbia	0.5			
Payments to States and counties from Forest Service receipts	0.4			
Payments to States from receipts under Mineral Leasing Act	0.5			
Payments to States and counties from Federal land management activities	0.2			
Payments in lieu of taxes	0.1			
Payments to territories and Puerto Rico	0.2			
Other	<u>0.3</u>			
Subtotal	2.2			
Other general government:				
Compacts of free association	0.2			
Territories	0.1			
Treasury claims	<u>0.5</u>			
Subtotal	0.8			
Deductions for Offsetting Receipts	-0.4			
TOTAL	**10.7**			

EXPENDITURE CATEGORIES	ACTUAL EXPENDITURES ($ Billions)	SPENDING CUTS		
		1	2	3
18. NET INTEREST:				
Interest on the public debt	264.8	_____	_____	_____
Interest received by on-budget trust funds	-46.4	_____	_____	_____
Other interest received	-18.2	_____	_____	_____
TOTAL	**200.2**	_____	_____	_____
19. UNDISTRIBUTED OFFSETTING RECEIPTS:				
On-budget only	-31.0	_____	_____	_____
TOTAL FEDERAL EXPENDITURES (on -budget only)	**1,026.6**	_____	_____	_____

RECEIPT CATEGORIES	ACTUAL RECEIPTS ($ Billions)	REVENUE ENHANCEMENTS		
		1	2	3

RECEIPTS:

21. INDIVIDUAL INCOME TAXES	466.9	_____	_____	_____
22. CORPORATION INCOME TAXES	93.5	_____	_____	_____
23. SOCIAL INSURANCE TAXES AND CONTRIBUTIONS:				
Employment taxes and contributions: Hospital insurance	68.6	_____	_____	_____
Railroad retirement: Social security equivalent account	1.4	_____	_____	_____
Rail pension fund	2.3	_____	_____	_____
Subtotal	3.7	_____	_____	_____
Subtotal	72.2	_____	_____	_____
Unemployment insurance	21.6	_____	_____	_____
Other retirement contributions: Federal employees retirement - employee contributions	4.4	_____	_____	_____
Contributions for non-Federal employees	0.1	_____	_____	_____
Subtotal	4.5	_____	_____	_____
TOTAL	**98.4**	_____	_____	_____

RECEIPT CATEGORIES	ACTUAL RECEIPTS ($ Billions)	REVENUE ENHANCEMENTS		
		1	2	3

24. EXCISE TAXES:

Alcohol taxes:

Distilled spirits	3.8			
Beer	1.7			
Wines	0.3			
Special taxes in connection with liquor occupations	0.1			
Refunds	-0.2			
Subtotal	5.7			

Tobacco taxes:

Cigarettes	4.0			
Net other receipts and refunds	0.1			
Subtotal	4.1			

Manufacturers' excise taxes:

Firearms, shells, and cartridges	0.1			
Gas guzzler	0.1			
Subtotal	0.2			

Miscellaneous excise taxes:

Telephone	3.0			
Employee pension plans	0.2			
Tax on foundations	0.2			
Foreign insurance policies	0.1			
Ozone depletion tax	0.4			
Subtotal	3.8			

Undistributed Federal tax deposits and unapplied collections	1.8			

EXCISE TAXES CONTINUED ON NEXT PAGE

RECEIPT CATEGORIES	ACTUAL RECEIPTS ($ Billions)	REVENUE ENHANCEMENTS		
		1	2	3

24. EXCISE TAXES (continued):

Highway Trust Fund:

Gasoline	9.4	___	___	___
Trucks, buses, and trailers	1.1	___	___	___
Tires, innertubes, and tread rubber	0.3	___	___	___
Diesel fuel used on highways	3.2	___	___	___
Use-tax on certain vehicles	0.6	___	___	___
Net other receipts and refunds	-0.7	___	___	___
Subtotal	13.9	___	___	___

Airport and airway:

Transportation of persons	3.2	___	___	___
Waybill tax	0.2	___	___	___
Tax on fuels	0.1	___	___	___
International departure tax	0.2	___	___	___
Subtotal	3.7	___	___	___

Aquatic resources trust fund	0.2	___	___	___
Black lung disability insurance trust fund	0.7	___	___	___
Inland waterway trust fund	0.1	___	___	___
Hazardous substance superfund	0.8	___	___	___
Oil spill liability trust fund	0.1	___	___	___
Vaccine injury compensation trust fund	0.2	___	___	___
Leaking underground storage tank trust fund	0.1	___	___	___
TOTAL	**35.3**	___	___	___

25. ESTATE AND GIFT TAXES	11.5	___	___	___
26. CUSTOMS DUTIES AND FEES	16.7	___	___	___
27. MISCELLANEOUS RECEIPTS	27.3	___	___	___
TOTAL RECEIPTS	**749.7**	___	___	___

SUMMARY

	SPENDING CUTS		
EXPENDITURE CATEGORIES	**1**	**2**	**3**
1. NATIONAL DEFENSE	_____	_____	_____
2. GENERAL SCIENCE, SPACE, AND TECHNOLOGY	_____	_____	_____
3. INTERNATIONAL AFFAIRS	_____	_____	_____
4. ENERGY	_____	_____	_____
5. AGRICULTURE	_____	_____	_____
6. NATURAL RESOURCES AND ENVIRONMENT	_____	_____	_____
7. COMMERCE AND HOUSING CREDIT	_____	_____	_____
8. TRANSPORTATION	_____	_____	_____
9. EDUCATION, TRAINING, EMPLOYMENT, AND SOCIAL SERVICES	_____	_____	_____
10. COMMUNITY AND REGIONAL DEVELOPMENT	_____	_____	_____
11. HEALTH	_____	_____	_____
12. INCOME SECURITY	_____	_____	_____
13. VETERANS BENEFITS AND SERVICES	_____	_____	_____
14. SOCIAL SECURITY	_____	_____	_____
15. MEDICARE	_____	_____	_____
16. ADMINISTRATION OF JUSTICE	_____	_____	_____
17. GENERAL GOVERNMENT	_____	_____	_____
18. NET INTEREST	_____	_____	_____
19. UNDISTRIBUTED OFFSETTING RECEIPTS	_____	_____	_____
TOTAL SAVINGS IN EXPENDITURES	_____	_____	_____

SUMMARY

| | REVENUE ENHANCEMENTS | | |
RECEIPT CATEGORIES	1	2	3
21. INDIVIDUAL INCOME TAX	____	____	____
22. CORPORATION INCOME TAX	____	____	____
23. SOCIAL SECURITY	____	____	____
24. EXCISE TAXES	____	____	____
25. ESTATE AND GIFT TAXES	____	____	____
26. CUSTOMS DUTIES AND FEES	____	____	____
27. MISCELLANEOUS RECEIPTS	____	____	____
TOTAL ADDITIONAL RECEIPTS	____	____	____

THE RECONCILIATION:

BEGINNING DEFICIT	$277 B	$277 B	$277 B
ADD: NEW REVENUES	____	____	____
ADD: EXPENDITURE SAVINGS	____	____	____
TOTAL	____	____	____

CONCLUSION

TIME FOR A CHANGE

Any Government, like any family, can for a year spend a little more than it earns. But you and I know that a continuation of that habit means the poorhouse.

Franklin D. Roosevelt

The Federal Government is huge, and growing - in fiscal year 1992, Federal spending will represent 25% of GNP. Massive deficits have become the norm, rather than the exception. The Federal budget deficit will reach a record high in fiscal year 1991. By all accounts, it is projected to exceed $300 billion, and will probably do so by a substantial margin. After years of promises, we have failed to move beyond the starting point toward deficit reduction. Now, more than ever before, it is time for a courageous and comprehensive solution to the budget imbalance.

There are only two ways to close the budget gap and repair the financial condition of the Government - one is to raise taxes, and the other is to reduce expenditures. But even today, faced with almost insurmountable deficits, the direction in which some elected officials would like to move is exactly the opposite. Smoothly crafted oratories continue to be made in support of spending increases for a myriad of programs. Alarming discussion drags on incessantly concerning the need for tax cuts. There are movements afoot for reductions in income taxes,

Social Security taxes (FICA), and the capital gains tax. All proposals for spending increases and tax cuts, in the current environment, go against conventional financial wisdom and sound accounting practices.

In the 1980s, "leveraged-buyouts" were common transactions. In a way, they reflected a society fascinated by and addicted to credit. Fast-talking financiers bought publicly-traded companies by taking on debt to finance the purchases. In many cases, the resulting companies were so burdened with debt obligations of interest and principal that they nearly went bankrupt. Fortunately, some of these leveraged-buyouts have since recovered by reselling stock equity to the public through the stock markets, using the proceeds to reduce the mountains of debt and relieve interest obligations.

The Federal Government cannot sell stock to finance a repurchase of its debt. Even if it could, few investors would be likely to purchase, given the poor "management team" which the Government has in place. The accumulated national debt is so large that each year a significant portion of tax revenues raised are used simply to pay interest on the debt. It is a burden to our government as much as an overused credit card is a burden to a frenetic shopper. In a very real way, the Government has reached its credit limit - more borrowing is counterproductive.

The programs and operations of the Federal Government are in need of a complete overhaul. Defense, Social Security, Medicare, and most other programs are ripe for reform. As citizens, we are the stockholders of the national government, and the stakeholders. Our management team (the Executive Branch) and our Board of Directors (Congress) need to get the message loud and clear: balance the budget now, make the necessary reforms, and manage for Federal financial security. Just as executives in the business world are replaceable, so too in the world of government are politicians and bureaucrats.

APPENDIX A

NOTE ON STATISTICS AND
FEDERAL ACCOUNTING PRACTICES

Most of the statistics used in this book have been compiled and reported by the some office or agency of the Federal Government. Whenever possible, the most recently available statistics were used. Many of the statistics were taken from the tables included in the budgets prepared by the Office of Management and Budget for Fiscal Years 1991 and 1992. Additional statistics were provided by the Department of Commerce, Bureau of the Census, Congressional Budget Office, Social Security Administration, Bureau of Labor Statistics, and the Agency for International Development, among others. Some data were provided by Congressional committees.

Population statistics and projections were provided by the Bureau of the Census and the Social Security Administration. The population statistic used in this book for 1990 is 250 million, which is between the actual count recorded by the Census Bureau and the amount which the Bureau projects through demographic analysis. Population forecasts for future years were taken from estimates by the Social Security Administration. The SSA has several population growth scenarios; in this book the middle, Alternative II-B scenario is used, and is referred to as the SSA *intermediate* projection. Social Security revenue and expenditure forecasts are also drawn from Alternative II-B projections.

Several accounting procedures and reporting changes are worthy of mention to facilitate a better understanding of the material presented in this book. They are as follows:

The Transition Quarter

The Transition Quarter accommodates the change in reporting periods used by the Federal Government. In 1976, the Government changed its accounting, or fiscal year. Prior to that year, Federal finances were accrued on a July 1 - June 30 time frame. Beginning in 1976, the fiscal year of the Federal Government changed to an October 1 - September 30 time frame. For historical recordkeeping, this change left three months, July - September 1976, officially unattached to any fiscal year. These months are known collectively as the Transition Quarter, or simply TQ. Most Federal statistics report the Transition Quarter separately. In this book, the Transition Quarter is usually included with Fiscal Year 1976, such that the fiscal 1976 reporting period is a non-standard 15 months (July 1, 1975 - September 30, 1976). Consequently, some graphs in this book exhibit a small upward spike for 1976 that deviates from an otherwise smoothly increasing trend line.

Federal Funds vs. Trust Funds

For accounting purposes, the Federal budget is separated into two broad categories: Federal funds and trust funds.

The majority of revenues and expenditures flow through the Federal funds accounts. The largest part of the Federal funds area is the General fund, which includes most income tax receipts and a large proportion of Federal outlays. Federal funds are generally unrestricted, and can be used for most any Government purpose.

Trust funds are quite different from Federal funds. A number of trust funds have been set up by the Government to fill particular needs. These trust funds typically have as a revenue source a special tax that has been established by the Government. The revenue collected by each trust fund through its tax is then used to provide a specific benefit or service. The largest Federal trust fund is the Old Age and Survivors Insurance Trust Fund (Social Security). It receives revenues through the FICA payroll tax, and disburses money to beneficiaries through monthly benefit checks.

On-Budget vs. Off-Budget

The on-budget/off-budget game became popular in the 1980s, as the Federal Government struggled to meet Gramm-Rudman deficit targets. Essentially, the core issue is whether or not a particular revenue and expense stream is included in the overall deficit calculations, which are used to measure progress against deficit targets. Since 1989, the operations of the U.S. Postal Service have been legally off-budget. The Gramm-Rudman legislation moved the revenues and expenditures of the two Social Security trust funds (the Old Age and Survivors Insurance Trust Fund and the Disability Insurance Trust Fund) off-budget, but allowed them to be included in the calculations which determined whether the Gramm-Rudman deficit targets were being met. The Omnibus Budget Reconciliation Act of 1990 reaffirmed the off-budget position of Social Security, and further mandated that the two trust funds be excluded from the deficit calculations. All other Federal activities are reported as on-budget.

APPENDIX B

CONGRESSIONAL CONNECTIONS

Never underestimate the power of the voting public. When important legislation comes before the House and Senate, the offices of Senators and Representatives are flooded with phone calls and letters supporting one side of an issue or the other. Members closely monitor the sentiment at home, and often vote to build credibility and popular support for help in the next election. If you aren't sure who represents you in Congress, call your local town or city hall.

The deficit and accumulated debt of the Federal Government are items worthy of your and your Members' time and attention. There are three easy ways for you to communicate with your elected representation in Congress:

1. Write to your Senators and your Representative.

    For Members of the House, write to:
        The Honorable _____
        United States House of Representatives
        Washington, DC 20515

    For Senators, write to:
        Senator _____
        United States Senate
        Washington, DC 20510

2. Telephone your Senators and Representative.

   Call the switchboard operator at the U.S. Capitol and ask for the Member's office. The switchboard number is (202) 224-3121.

3. Visit your Senators and Representative.

   Schedule an appointment with your Member at his or her local office in your area. Or if you plan to visit Washington, D.C. when Congress is in session, call the Member's Capitol Hill office and schedule an appointment in advance.

BIBLIOGRAPHY

Aaron, Henry J., and Harvey Galper. Assessing Tax Reform. Washington, D.C.: The Brookings Institution, 1985.

Agency for International Development. Fiscal Year 1991 Congressional Presentation. March 1990.

Agency for International Development. Fiscal Year 1992 Congressional Presentation. March 1991.

Bacon, Kenneth H., and Bruce Ingersoll. "Budget Package Will Slow Entitlement Appropriations by About $100 Billion." Wall Street Journal, October 26, 1990, p. A4.

Balz, Dan. "Raises Set For Federal Executives." Washington Post, December 13, 1990, p. A1.

Becker, Gary S. "Your Tax Dollars Are At Work - On the Wrong Jobs." Business Week, November 26, 1990, p. 18.

Begley, Sharon, and Mary Hager. "Park-Barrel Politics." Newsweek, November 26, 1990, pp. 60-62.

Berry, John M., and Steven Mufson. "Budget Plan Puts Fed in Interest-Rate Bind." Washington Post, October 29, 1990, p. A1.

Bettner, Jill. "More Taxpayers Face Alternative Minimum." Wall Street Journal, October 29, 1990, p. C16.

Birnbaum, Jeffrey H. "Budget Plan Doesn't Include A Tax Increase." Wall
    Street Journal, April 9, 1991, p. A3.

Birnbaum, Jeffrey H.   "Huge Tax Increase Measure Does Contain Some
    Breaks." Wall Street Journal, October 26, 1990, p. A4.

Birnbaum, Jeffrey H., and Jackie Calmes. "Budget Talks Stall on Taxes For
    the Wealthy." Wall Street Journal, October 22, 1990, p. A3.

Birnbaum, Jeffrey H., and Jackie Calmes. "Corporate Rate Increase to 35%
    is Suggested." Wall Street Journal, October 23, 1990, p. A3.

Birnbaum, Jeffrey H., and Jackie Calmes. "Lawmakers Set Budget Plan And
    Predict Its Approval." Wall Street Journal, October 25, 1990, p. A3.

Brittain, John A. The Payroll Tax for Social Security. Washington, D.C.:
    The Brookings Institution, 1972.

Bureau of the Public Debt, Department of the Treasury. Monthly Statement
    of the Public Debt of the United States. September 30, 1990.

Bureau of the Public Debt, Department of the Treasury. Monthly Statement
    of the Public Debt of the United States. December 31, 1990.

Calmes, Jackie. "Payroll-Tax Cut, Supported by Liberals And Conservatives,
    Again Is a Big Issue." Wall Street Journal, February 8, 1991, p. A2.

Calmes, Jackie, and Jeffrey H. Birnbaum.   "Lawmakers Try To Complete
    Budget Accord." Wall Street Journal, October 26, 1990, p. A3.

Committee on Foreign Affairs, U.S. House of Representatives. Report of the
    Task Force on Foreign Assistance to the Committee on Foreign Affairs,
    U.S. House of Representatives.   Washington: U.S. Government
    Printing Office, 1989.

Committee on Ways and Means, U.S. House of Representatives. Overview
    of Entitlement Programs: 1990 Green Book.   Washington: U.S.
    Government Printing Office, 1990.

Committee on Ways and Means, U.S. House of Representatives. Overview
    of the Federal Tax System. Washington: U.S. Government Printing
    Office, 1990.

"Comparing the Two Tax Bills." New York Times, July 29, 1981, p. D13.

Congressional Budget Office. The Economic and Budget Outlook: Fiscal
    Years 1991-1995. January 1990.

Congressional Budget Office. The Economic and Budget Outlook: Fiscal Years 1992-1996. January 1991.

Congressional Budget Office. The 1990 Budget Agreement: An Interim Assessment. December 1990.

Cowan, Edward. "48 Democrats Join 190 House Republicans to Defeat Party's Bill." New York Times, July 30, 1981, p. A1.

Daggett, Stephen and Gary J. Pagliano. Persian Gulf War: U.S. Costs and Allied Financial Contributions. Congressional Research Service, March 11, 1991.

Devroy, Ann. "Bush Threatens Veto If Congress Tries to Regain Power to Estimate Budget Costs." Washington Post, December 22, 1990, p. A4.

"Do Nothing, Congress." Washington Post, January 24, 1991, p. A20.

Farney, Dennis. "Reagan's Mastery of Economic Policies In Congress May Sag on Social Issues." Wall Street Journal, July 30, 1981, p. 3.

Fetterman, Mindy, and Michelle Osborn. "Financial cost for a day at war: $500 million." USA Today, January 18, 1991, p. B1.

"Fortune 500 Largest U.S. Industrial Corporations." Fortune, April 23, 1990, pp. 346-367.

Friedman, Benjamin M. Day of Reckoning. New York: Random House, 1988.

Fromson, Brett Duval. "Will the FDIC Run Out of Money." Fortune, October 8, 1990, pp. 119-127.

Galbraith, John Kenneth, and Paul W. McCracken. Reaganomics: Meaning, Means, and Ends. New York: The Free Press, 1983.

Gleckman, Howard, Paula Dwyer, and Mike McNamee. "The Last Best Chance?" Business Week, October 15, 1990, pp. 24-27.

Gleckman, Howard, Vicky Cahan, and Paula Dwyer. "A Tax Here, A Tax There - Pretty Soon, It's Real Money." Business Week, October 15, 1990, pp. 28-29.

Greenberger, Robert S. "Estimates of Cost of War Against Iraq Range From $17 Billion to $80 Billion." Wall Street Journal, January 23, 1991, p. A2.

Greenwald, John. "No End in Sight." Time, August 13, 1990, pp. 50-52.

Kenworthy, Tom. "Kansan Targets Pork Barrel Projects." Washington Post, December 19, 1990, p. A21.

Knight, Jerry. "Regulators Are Moving to Extend Federal Insurance for Credit Unions." Washington Post, January 24, 1991, p. E1.

"Major Provisions of Two Bills Cover Individuals, Businesses." New York Times, July 30, 1981, p. D20.

McKenzie, Richard B. "The Retreat of the Elderly Welfare State." Wall Street Journal, March 12, 1991, p. A18.

Meehan, John et al. "A Shock to the System." Business Week, January 21, 1991, pp. 24-26.

Merry, Robert W. "Congress Clears Reagan's Tax-Cut Plan, Rejecting Traditional Economic Policies." Wall Street Journal, July 30, 1981, p. 3.

Mossberg, Walter S. "High-Tech, Low-Casualty Success in War So Far Owes Much to Jimmy Carter's Defense Planning." Wall Street Journal, January 22, 1991, p. A16.

Mufson, Steven. "$50 Billion Added to Deficit Forecast." Washington Post, January 8, 1991, p. A1.

Mufson, Steven, and John E. Yang. "Congress Set To Tackle Issue of War's Cost." Washington Post, January 24, 1991, p. E1.

Murray, Alan, and David Wessel. "Budget Follies: Deficit Plan Emerges, But at a Heavy Cost In Public Confidence." Wall Street Journal, October 26, 1990, p. A1.

Office of Management and Budget. Budget of the United States Government, Fiscal Year 1991. Washington: U.S. Government Printing Office, 1990.

Office of Management and Budget. Budget of the United States Government, Fiscal Year 1992. Washington: U.S. Government Printing Office, 1991.

Oreskes, Michael. "Advantage: Democrats." New York Times, October 29, 1990, p. A1.

Organisation for Economic Cooperation and Development. Development Cooperation in the 1990s. December 1989.

Pear, Robert. "Most Americans To Feel Impact Of Deficit Plan," New York Times, October 28, 1990, p. A1.

Palmer, John L., and Isabel V. Sawhill, eds. The Reagan Record, Cambridge, Massachusetts: Ballinger Publishing Company, 1984.

Paulos, John Allen. Innumeracy: Mathematical Illiteracy and Its Consequences. New York: Vintage Books, 1990.

Public Law 98-21: Social Security Amendments of 1983. 98th Congress of the United States, April 20, 1983.

Public Law 99-177: The Balanced Budget and Emergency Deficit Control Act of 1985. 99th Congress of the United States, December 12, 1985.

Public Law 100-119. The Balanced Budget and Emergency Deficit Control Reaffirmation Act of 1987. 100th Congress of the United States, September 29, 1987.

Public Law 101-73. Financial Institutions Reform, Recovery, and Enforcement Act of 1989. 101st Congress of the United States, August 9, 1989.

Reagan, Ronald R. "The Text of Reagan's Speech Comparing the Details of Tax Cut Proposals." New York Times, July 28, 1981, p. B6.

Reischauer, Robert D. Testimony on the CBO's Interim Assessment of the Economic and Budget Outlook before the Committee on the Budget, U.S. House of Representatives, December 6, 1990.

Rich, Spencer. "Social Security and Fairness: Should Tax Rate Be Cut?" Washington Post, February 18, 1991, p. A23.

Rich, Spencer. "Who Needs Medicaid?" Washington Post, January 6, 1991, p. C3.

Rogers, David. "Pentagon Budget Receives Final Approval in House." Wall Street Journal, October 26, 1990, p. A4.

Rogers, David. "Spending Bills Reflect Revamped Budget For Defense, Shift to Domestic Programs." Wall Street Journal, October 22, 1990, p. A3.

Rosenbaum, David E. "House, 228 to 200, Sends Budget Bill on to Senate Vote," New York Times, October 28, 1990, p. A1.

Samuelson, Robert J.   "Lure of the Free Lunch."   Washington Post, November 15, 1990, p. A25.

Samuelson, Robert J.   "Pampering the Elderly (II)."   Newsweek, November 26, 1990, p. 58.

Schmedel, Scott R.   "Taxpayers' Choices Narrow as Deductions Thin."   Wall Street Journal, October 29, 1990, p. C1.

Schmedel, Scott R., and Mark N. Dodosh.   "Accountants Expect Tax Bill to Cause Big Changes in Investment Strategies."   Wall Street Journal, July 31, 1981, p. 4.

Schmidt, Susan.   "Fed Seeks Quick Fix for Credit Crunch."   Washington Post, January 24, 1991, p. E1.

Seidman, L. William.   Testimony on Resolution Trust Corporation Funding Issues before the Committee on Banking, Finance and Urban Affairs, U.S. House of Representatives, July 30, 1990.

Seidman, L.William.   Testimony on Resolution Trust Corporation Funding Issues before the Committee on Ways and Means, U.S. House of Representatives, September 19, 1990.

Silk, Leonard.   "Radically New Course For U.S. Fiscal Policy."   New York Times, July 30, 1981, p. A1.

Smith, Hedrick.   "The President Attains Mastery at the Capitol."   New York Times, July 30, 1981, p. A1.

Stein, Herbert.   Presidential Economics.   New York: Simon and Schuster, 1984.

Strudler, Michael and Emily Ring.   "Individual Income Tax Returns, Preliminary Data, 1988."   U.S. Department of the Treasury Statistics of Income Bulletin, Volume 9, No. 4, Spring 1990.

Stockman, David A.   The Triumph of Politics.   New York: Harper and Row, 1986.

"Tax-Cut Picture Clears, But Effect on Economy Remains Very Cloudy."   Wall Street Journal, July 31, 1981, p. 1.

The Board of Trustees of the Federal Old Age and Survivors Insurance and Disability Insurance Trust Funds.   The 1990 Annual Report of the

Federal Old Age and Survivors Insurance and Disability Insurance Trust Funds. Washington: U.S. Government Printing Office, 1990.

The Board of Trustees of the Federal Supplementary Medical Insurance Trust Fund. 1990 Annual Report of the Board of Trustees of the Federal Supplementary Medical Insurance Trust Fund. Washington: U.S. Government Printing Office, 1990.

"The Deficit Shell." Wall Street Journal, October 23, 1990, p. A18.

The Federal Hospital Insurance Trust Fund. The 1989 Annual Report of the Board of Trustees of the Federal Hospital Insurance Trust Fund. Washington: U.S. Government Printing Office, 1990.

Thomas, Paulette. "House Approves S&L Bailout Bill of $78 Billion." Wall Street Journal, March 14, 1991, p. A3.

U.S. Bureau of the Census. Statistical Abstract of the United States: 1990. Washington: U.S. Government Printing Office, 1990.

U.S. Department of Commerce. Census Bureau Releases Preliminary Coverage Estimates From the Post-Enumeration Survey and Demographic Analysis. News Release: April 18, 1991.

U.S. Department of Commerce. State Personal Income, Fourth Quarter 1990 and Per Capita Personal Income, 1990. News Release: April 17, 1991.

U.S. House of Representatives. Conference Report to Accompany H.R. 5835: Omnibus Budget Reconciliation Act of 1990, Report 101-964. Washington: U.S. Government Printing Office, 1990.

U.S. Office of Personnel Management. Federal Civilian Workforce Statistics: Employment and Trends as of September 1990.

Weisman, Steven R. "President Signs Economic Program With A Warning." New York Times, August 14, 1981, p. A1.

Wessel, David. "Cutting the Deficit: Evolution of a Deal." Wall Street Journal, October 26, 1990, p. A4.

Wessel, David. "The U.S. Spent $31.5 Billion On Gulf War." Wall Street Journal, April 30, 1991, p. A26.

Wessel, David, and Jackie Calmes. "GOP Budget Revolt May Be Backfiring As Democrats Gain Leverage on Bush." Wall Street Journal, October 23, 1990, p. A6.

Yang, John E. "Panel Votes $16 Billion for War Costs." Washington <u>Post</u>, March 15, 1991, p. A14.

Yang, John E. "Weary Lawmakers Pass Fiscal Package: Bush Says He'll Sign 5-Year Deficit Plan." Washington <u>Post</u>, October 28, 1990, p. A1.

Yang, John E, and Steven Mufson. "Package Termed Best Circumstances Permit." Washington <u>Post</u>, October 29, 1990, p. A1.

INDEX

Government in Crisis - What Every American Should Know About the Federal Budget Deficit is published by Chesapeake River Press. Additional copies can be obtained by using the order form below.

....

BOOK ORDER FORM

Please send me _____ copy(ies) of
**GOVERNMENT IN CRISIS - WHAT EVERY
AMERICAN SHOULD KNOW ABOUT THE FEDERAL
BUDGET DEFICIT** @ $9.95 each $_____

Virginia residents add 4.5% sales tax ($.45 per book) $_____

Postage and Handling to U.S. Addresses: $2.00 per book $_____

TOTAL DUE $_____

Please send this order form with your check,
made payable to Chesapeake River Press.

Name_____
Street_____
City_____
State_____ Zip_____

Mail this form, along with payment to:

    Chesapeake River Press
    P.O. Box 19141
    Alexandria, Virginia 22320

For discounts on large quantity orders of ten copies or more, write to us at the address above.